The Parable of White Fang

Based on the Classic Jack London Novel

By
David G. Smithson, MD

Copyright © 2021 David G. Smithson, MD
All rights reserved.

ISBN: 978-1-7374150-2-2

Dedication

To the Curé of Ars

Contents

Preface i
Introduction 1
Chapter 1: Living For Today 5
Chapter 2: Filled With Awe 12
Chapter 3: A Painful Lesson 17
Chapter 4: The Ancient Covenant 23
Chapter 5: The Cage of Horror 30
Chapter 6: The Love Begins 37
Chapter 7: The Dark Night 51
Chapter 8: Enemy Combat 59
Chapter 9: A New Land 64
Chapter 10: Purposeful Temptation 77
Chapter 11: Random Temptation 80
Chapter 12: The Walls Come Down 83
Chapter 13: Scenes of Life 88
Chapter 14: Joyful Triumph 95
Notes 99
Author Biography 101
Acknowledgments 103

Preface

With the coronavirus pandemic of 2020, our world changed like never before. Governmental mandates, stores closing up shop, society essentially shutting down and moving on-line. In the early days of the pandemic, no one was out and traffic on the roadways became sparse. At the hospital I worked at, we were continually monitoring the COVID-19 numbers. How many positives? How many on ventilators? Being a rehabilitation medicine physician, I had previously directed the care of patients after a stroke, amputation or brain injury, but now this list included patients who were recovering from the coronavirus. Patients who had been critically ill or on the ventilator and were very weak and debilitated. Some of them could not stand or walk and needed physical rehabilitation.

At home, my wife's business as a personal health consultant became even busier than normal as people were obviously more concerned regarding their health. Our youngest daughter was living at home and her college curriculum was moved to online. With the coronavirus shut down, all social activities were cancelled. Our social calendar all of a sudden became blank. No outings in the evening. Nothing was open. We couldn't even go to church as it was virtual. We all started getting used to a different way of living.

With my wife and daughter busy with their own pursuits, the crisis driven coronavirus filled media was not of interest to me, especially with my living with the results of it during the day. I considered my options. I actually had some time on my hands, time I had not previously anticipated. I went downstairs to my library. Were there any books I wanted to read growing up and was not able to? Any classics I had always wanted to consume? Maybe some lighter fare to offset the heaviness of our current conditions? I first spent my evenings reading old Reader's Digest condensed versions including *Treasure Island* (1) and *David Copperfield* (2). I then read the classic *The Call of the Wild* (3) by Jack London and really enjoyed the adventure. Knowing I had another book about dogs that I had never read from my grandfather, I was again browsing in my library. After a period of time I found it, in the far corner of the wall of the library shielded by a larger book. It was an aged, weathered book with yellowed pages, copywrite 1906. It was called *White Fang* and was also written by Jack London (4).

So I started spending my evenings on the back patio, bringing my golden retriever, Chloe, along with me. She would lay at my side as I would read about another dog, (part wolf, part wild dog) being raised in the wilds of the Yukon by the name of White Fang. I would look past our barn and past the orchard into the untamed wooded area and creek bed beyond our property. Would the Yukon wilds look anything like that? As I read, there were certain quotes that almost jumped off the page. I needed to take note. There were analogies and similarities that were striking. It was as if I was actually reading two stories simultaneously. This book was not just about the relationship between man and dog. It was about more, much more. It was becoming apparent to me that this book was about the deeper relationship between God and man.

One evening, when I was nearing the end of the book, I went out onto the back patio with Chloe as usual. Chloe was laying at my side and I was engrossed with the book. Suddenly Chloe stood up and was in rapt attention looking out into the backyard. When I looked out at where Chloe was looking, there I saw it. It was a large coyote. Grayish-white with a touch of brown. In our 20 years living on the property, I had never seen a coyote like this. Only once had I seen another coyote, but it was much smaller. We have plenty of red foxes and deer, and many other wild creatures, but never a coyote like this. It was large with long legs, and it stood still, looking at us. For several seconds, we stared at each other. No one moved. Then Chloe made a move to run out after it, and I called Chloe's name. At that the coyote took off, swiftly moving, with its long legs almost looking wolf like. It glided gracefully around the orchard, past the barn, out into the untamed wooded area, out into the wild.

I hope you enjoy this journey. It is a journey that involves not only man and dog, but also God and man. As we shall see, it is a surprisingly similar journey.

INTRODUCTION

In the book *Making Sense Out of Suffering* by Peter Kreeft (5), there is a back and forth dialogue between the author and the supposed reader regarding the larger question of suffering and why there is suffering in the first place. In the discussion, Kreeft makes use of an analogy involving the relationship of God and man to that of man and dog. The discussion picks up as follows:

> Author: … Like the goodness of a dog and the goodness of a man – they are different but not wholly different. "Good doggy" means the dog has some qualities that we call good in a man, too; loyalty and affection, for instance. But the man also has qualities the dog can't have. God is to us something like what we are to a dog.
> Reader: How does this apply to suffering now?
> Author: A hunter sometimes makes his dog suffer – for instance when the dog is caught in a trap, the hunter has to push the dog further into the trap to less the tension on it before he can get him out. That hurts and if the dog were a theologian it would probably question the dogma of the goodness of man because it can't understand

what we can: the mechanism of a trap requires this push further in that causes such pain because this is the way out. God does the same to us sometimes, and we can't understand why he does it any more than the dog can understand us.
Reader: We are stuck then.
Author: No, we can trust him as the dog can trust its master.
Reader: What difference does it make?
Author: If we trust, we won't scream and pull and rebel and make it harder to get out …

In the above discussion, Kreeft makes the point that "God is to us something like what we are to a dog." He talks about the analogy of these two relationships and how there are certain similarities. It is these similarities and this very concept which is the basis of this book. It is not the cutesy story of a fluffy doggie whose antics cause us superficial delight. No, this book digs deeper. Much deeper.

This book is based on the classic Jack London novel *White Fang*. *White Fang* is the story of a wolf/wild dog named White Fang, born and raised in the Yukon wild with wolves. He was initially captured and tamed by his first owner and used as a sled dog, guard dog and human companion. His next owner, unfortunately, abused and maltreated him, using him in illegal dog fights with the result that he became nothing short of a vicious beast. The story then takes us on the long and difficult process of White Fang being gradually re-tamed and eventually domesticated by a new, extremely patient, and very loving owner.

In this book we look at the relationship between God and man with some insights learned from the above story's relationship between man and dog. It attempts to see our faith from a different perspective; it is not meant to be a dry doctrinal text but instead considers thought-provoking and even unexpected aspects of our faith within the story. It covers multiple challenging topics and attempts to look at them from this different vantage point. Some of the many topics discussed include: the ancient covenant, the new covenant, the awe of God, suffering and abuse, the reality of evil, the reality of love, laws of obedience, expiation, redemption and salvation, heaven, temptation and the spiritual battle, the dark night of the soul, learned restraint, examination of conscience, role of conscience, stain of sin, confession/reconciliation, imperfect versus perfect contrition, holy leisure, expression not repression and the process of taming versus the process of growing in holiness. Other topics include the nature of God, the nature of man and the nature of animal. And yes, all of this involving a wild wolf dog!

Each chapter is arranged into two major sections. The first section is in standard print and includes background information and direct quotes in bold print from Jack London's *White Fang*. The second section is in italics and is a contemplation which I compile discussing the issues raised in the first section. Some chapters have more than one contemplation, again referring to the initial section, and some have endnotes. These contemplations discuss spiritual dimensions between God and man as analogous to the relationship between man and dog.

DAVID G. SMITHSON, MD

In the end, this book tells a story of love. A deep, enduring, life changing, other centered, compassionate, mutually joyful and triumphant love. This love involves not only man and dog but also God and man.

Please enjoy the read!

CHAPTER 1

LIVING FOR TODAY

The classic book *White Fang* was written in 1906 by Jack London. It is set in the frigid Yukon wilderness and the opening chapters give a dramatic representation of the extreme cold, remoteness and desolation of the northland. All types of life struggle just to survive. There are dark spruce forests covered in frost, frozen waterways and snow covered ground. The temperatures can reach 50 degrees below zero. To quote the author, **"It was the Wild, the savage, frozen-hearted, Northland Wild."**

The story gradually begins to follow a gaunt, starving wolf pack. They are looking for life, for some animal to kill, and things are desperate. One of the wolf pack is actually a previously tamed dog who is now living in its native wild habitat due to the extreme conditions. This dog is described as a **"she-wolf"** and is actually half wolf and half dog. We find out later that she had previously been domesticated by a tribe of native Indians living in the area and given the name "Kiche". It was during a famine that Kiche wandered from the Indian tribe and actually joined with this wolf pack and thus was functioning as a wild beast. As the story continues, the pack of wolves scour in near despair the frozen surroundings for any sight of life, for any potential living creature to kill and eat. Eventually they come upon a large 800-pound moose which they were able, as a group, to take down. For them, the famine was over as they gorged themselves.

The wolf pack then splits up and Kiche travels primarily with three other wolves, all male. These male wolves eventually fight each other to the death for her, until one wolf named "One Eye" remains. One Eye and Kiche then mate and travel together as a twosome. The temperatures begin to rise and the frozen wasteland begins to thaw as daylight hours increase. Signs of spring are emerging. Kiche searches out and finds a lair. It is here that she births six cubs. One Eye scours the land for food, but signs and trails of rabbit, squirrel or other living things are scarce. There is very little to bring back to the lair for Kiche and the cubs. Without meat, her milk supply dries up and all of the cubs die of starvation except for one, a gray cub. It is during this time that One Eye also is killed by a lynx. This leaves just the she-wolf Kiche and her little gray cub.

The story then takes the viewpoint of this young cub. As Kiche is out hunting for food, the adventuresome cub starts to wander out of the lair. He starts to explore his surroundings and gradually takes longer expeditions from the lair. He stumbles by accident during one of his outings into a nest of baby ptarmigans. First he is frightened, and then with his ingrained instinct, the cub's **"jaws closed ... and there was a crunching of fragile bones and warm blood ran from his mouth. The taste of it was good."**

The gray cub ends up eating the entire brood of baby birds and then as he is leaving the nest feeling proud as the conqueror, he is suddenly attacked by the ptarmigan hen. **"It was his first battle. He was elated ... He was no longer afraid of anything."** But he is still a small cub against a very angry hen, and he is about to lose the battle when by a stroke of luck a great hawk suddenly swoops down and snatches the mother ptarmigan and carries her away. The cub was thus saved at the last minute. It was through this that he learned a law of the wild: **"KILL OR BE KILLED"**.

As the story goes on, the cub grows and develops, but the famine continues upon the land and Kiche herself has problems finding any meat. The famine becomes so terrible that she is forced to raid the nest of the lynx knowing full well that the lynx is a vicious animal and will try to extract revenge. After she and the gray cub raid the nest and devour the kittens, the mother lynx finds out and indeed comes after them. While Kiche can fight the lynx with her teeth, the lynx also has all four claws and is both powerful and furious with her loss. It is a ferocious battle. When the young gray cub sinks his teeth into the hind leg of the lynx, this weakens her and enables Kiche and the gray cub together to overpower the lynx. From this, however, Kiche was wounded almost to the point of death and the cub's shoulder was ripped to the bone. Kiche and the cub then devour the lynx while recovering from their own injuries.

From this endeavor the gray cub learned yet another lesson. To further quote the author: **"The aim of life was meat. Life itself was meat. Life lived on life. There were the eaters and the eaten. The law was: EAT OR**

BE EATEN. He did not formulate the law in clear, set terms and moralize about it. He did not even think the law; he merely lived the law without thinking about it at all.

He saw the law operating around him on every side. He had eaten the ptarmigan chicks. The hawk would also have eaten him. Later, when he had grown more formidable, he wanted to eat the hawk. He had eaten the lynx kitten. The lynx-mother would have eaten him had she not herself been killed and eaten. And so it went. The law was being lived about him by all live things, and he himself was part and parcel of the law. He was a killer. His only food was meat, live meat, that ran away swiftly before him, or flew into the air, or climbed trees, or hid in the ground, or faced him and fought with him, or turned the tables and ran after him.

Had the cub thought in man-fashion, he might have epitomized life as a voracious appetite, and the world as a place wherein ranged a multitude of appetites, pursuing and being pursed, hunting and being hunted, eating and being eaten, all in blindness and confusion, with violence and disorder, a chaos of gluttony and slaughter, ruled over by chance, merciless, planless, endless.

But the cub did not think in man-fashion. He did not look at things with wide vision. He was single-purposed, and entertained but one thought or desire at a time. Besides the law of meat, there was a myriad other and lesser laws for him to learn and obey. The world was filled with surprise. The stir of the life that was in him, the play of his muscles, was an unending happiness. To run down meat was to experience thrills and elations. His rages and battles were pleasures. Terror itself, and the mystery of the unknown, lent to his living.

And there were easements and satisfactions. To have a full stomach, to doze lazily in the sunshine – such things were remuneration in full for his ardors and toils, while his ardors and toils were in themselves self-remunerative. They were expressions of life, and life is always happy when it is expressing itself. So the cub had no quarrel with his hostile environment. He was very much alive, very happy, and very proud of himself."

Contemplation

Jack London, the author of White Fang, *considered himself an atheist. When he was around 19 years of age, he was arrested for tramping and vagrancy. On the necessary forms during his arrest he listed "atheist" as his religion (6). Later in his adult life, he is quoted as saying, "I believe that when I am dead, I am dead. I believe that with my death I am just as much obliterated as the last mosquito you and I squashed." (7). He also was noted to be a naturalist writer and was thought to espouse the philosophical belief that everything arises from natural properties and causes and that supernatural factors are rejected. In this belief system, only natural laws and forces operate in the universe.*

We can see elements of this viewpoint in the above chapter quotations. The following paragraph noted above is especially telling: **"Had the cub thought in man** fashion, he might have epitomized life as a voracious appetite. The world is a place wherein raged a multitude of appetites pursing and being pursued, hunting and being hunted, eating and being eaten, all in blindness and confusion with violence and disorder. A chaos of gluttony and slaughter ruled over by chance, merciless, planless, endless." *The terms that he uses in this above paragraph including* "disorder… ruled over by chance, merciless, planless, endless" *have a pessimistic characteristic typical of naturalism and void of any type of supernatural influence. It describes a harsh environment where the characters are left alone to fight for their lives.*

Yet, if we transpose ourselves into the place of the gray cub above we can see some of this in our own lives. The old saying, "It's a dog eat dog world" comes to mind. This describes the fierce and at times ruthless behavior of some people in a competitive human world. It focuses on self-serving even if that means harming others. There is a viciousness inherent in it, a type of savagery.

There are many who live and have lived as if life were nothing more than being ruled over by chance, a world without mercy and without planning and seemingly without end. This is a world without meaning. The law of meat described above could be transitioned into "the law of pleasure" with respect to mankind, basic hedonism. If there is no supernatural reality and if life only exists in the here and now, then the focus is on maximizing the satisfaction of our desires. Once the basic desires and senses are satisfied, then it expands to the seeking of maximizing pleasure. Within this mindset there is a certain materialism and a focus on nothing more than what can be seen, touched, digested; a full satisfaction of the senses. In referencing back to White Fang *above:* **"To have a full stomach, to doze lazily in the sunshine – such things were remuneration in full for his ardors and toils …"** *This may be all that exists and has existed in the mindset for many. There is the focus on self, the focus on the material, the focus on pleasure without any reference to any type of supernatural existence. This is a carnal, base existence. There is no role and no sense to suffering as it just keeps us from fulfilling our basic wants and needs. And there is no real tomorrow, it is focused on just today. The old adage, "eat, drink and be merry, for tomorrow we die," sums up the thinking. There is no God, there is no higher plan, there is only the here and now and what we can get from it for ourselves.*

Chapter 2

Filled With Awe

The previous chapter initially focused on the challenges, dangers and experiences of a young cub surviving in the wilderness. In this chapter, the theme starts to change as the gray cub begins to learn an even more challenging undertaking: that of surviving in a civilized society. As we will see, he has to learn the challenges and difficulties of living among human beings.

As the story continues, the she-wolf Kiche and the gray cub happen upon some members of the Indian tribe that had previously tamed Kiche. The Indians call her out by name and the gray cub is astonished as his mother cowers to them, crouching down, whimpering, wagging her tail. The cub had difficulty understanding this. Yet he was awed by the man-animal creatures that were around them. When one of the man-animals tried to pick him up, he bristled and glared his teeth, finally biting the man-animal in the hand. From there proceeded a clout with a club on one side of his skull. This followed with a clout on the other side of his skull. The cub was both dazed and amazed. What power and what strength! A piece of wood that seemed to come out of nowhere was hitting him. It was then that the Indians named him "White Fang" because of the fangs that he displayed. With his mother being leashed and led back to the Indian camp, he had no choice but to go with her and the Indian man that laid claim to them both, an Indian by the name of "Gray Beaver".

As they were taken into the Indian camp, his sense of awe increased even more. There were many men and women and children, teepees, camp equipment, canoes. Also there were many dogs that lived in the camp. Upon initially coming into the camp these dogs rushed on White Fang and he felt fighting and slashing of teeth on his body as they surrounded him. There was a great uproar. He could hear the snarl of Kiche as she fought for him and he could hear the cries of the man-animals as they utilized their clubs in hitting the multiple dogs to get them away from White Fang.

The author describes this scene as follows: **"He could now see the man-animals driving back the dogs with clubs and stones, defending him, saving him from the savage teeth of his kind that somehow was not his kind. And though there was no reason in his brain for a clear conception of so abstract a thing as justice, nevertheless, in his own way, he felt the justice of the man-animals, and he knew them for what they were – makers of law and executors of law. Also, he appreciated the power with which they administered the law. Unlike any animals he had ever encountered, they did not bite nor claw. They enforced their live strength with the power of dead things. Dead things** did their bidding. Thus, sticks and stones, directed by these strange creatures, leaped through the air like living things, inflicting grievous hurts upon the dogs.'

White Fang was further astonished at the power and the abilities of these man creatures: "They were superior creatures, of a verity, gods. To his dim comprehension they were as much wonder -workers as gods are to men. They were creatures of mastery, possessing all manner of unknown and impossible potencies, overlords of the alive and the not alive-making obey that which moved, importing movement to that which did not move and making life, sun colored and biting life, to grow out of dead moss and wood. They were fire-makers. They were gods!"

It was beyond anything he had ever experienced: "To his mind this was power unusual, power inconceivable and beyond the natural, power that was god-like. White Fang, in the very nature of him, could never know anything about gods; at the best he could know only things that were beyond knowing; but the wonder and awe that he had of these man-animals in ways resembled what would be the wonder and awe of man at sight of some celestial creature, on a mountain top, hurling thunderbolts from either hand at an astonished world."

Contemplation

As White Fang looked in awe upon the man-animals with a power that was god-like, so, too, has mankind historically attributed god-like powers to the heavens and to our natural surroundings. Nature itself is awe-inspiring in many different ways. Examples of this could include the intricate beauty and fragrant smell of a delicate flower to the scenic views from a mountain overlook to the crashing waves of the vast oceans. Likewise, our own bodies can be sources of awe with the intricate working together of the bodily organs and cellular matter. The celestial bodies above resulting in a twinkling, stellar show on a cloudless night can be a source of awe. Furthermore, these examples illustrate not just awe-inspiring beauty but also power. Thunderbolts causing a jolt across the sky can amaze us with their might. Throughout our human history there has been a raising up of our eyes toward the heavens, a looking up at something that is greater than we are; a something that is incredible, complex, beautiful, dynamic, and appears beyond our understanding. From the laws of celestial bodies to the properties of a one-cellular organism, there is such organization, such impressive attention to each detail. It is thus not surprising that over our entire human history we have developed nature-gods, gods with which we can worship, gods that seem to help us in our understanding of things that are bigger than us. It is an innate desire in the search of something greater than ourselves, an attempt to understand this world that we live in and the reasons for our existence, those deep questions of ultimate meaning.

As we have learned more about the cosmos we have come to the realization that nature is incredibly fine-tuned to produce the universe we see. And this leads to further questions that have long troubled philosophers and theologians. Questions such as: Does the universe really go on forever, and has it always existed? Why are there such intricate mathematical laws that govern the universe, laws that we humans can access and figure out? And how did those laws get put in place? We can even ask more basic questions such as: Why does the universe exist at all? Instead of nothing, why is there something?

Albert Einstein is known to be one of the greatest scientists of all time. His studies engendered in him a sense of awe as can be seen in the following quote: "Everyone who is seriously involved in the pursuit of science becomes convinced that a spirit is manifest in the laws of the universe – a spirit vastly superior to that of man and one in the face of which we, with our modest powers, must feel humble." While Einstein didn't believe in a personal God he wasn't an atheist either as indicated in this further quote: "I believe in God – who reveals himself in the orderly harmony of the universe."

Sir Isaac Newton is also thought to be one of the greatest scientists of all time. He was a daily Bible reader and actually wrote more about issues of faith than science. He also was awe struck with the celestial findings he encountered: "The most beautiful system of the sun, planets and comets, could only proceed from the counsel and dominion of an intelligent and powerful being." He also is quoted: "Atheism is so senseless. When I look at the solar system, I see the earth is the right distance from the sun to receive the proper amount of heat and light. This did not happen by chance. The true God is a living, intelligent and powerful being."

As White Fang was awe struck by the man-animals that surrounded him so also can we be awe struck by the natural and celestial domain that surrounds us.

CHAPTER 3

A PAINFUL LESSON

While Kiche is leashed and tied up near Gray Beaver's teepee at the Indian camp, White Fang is allowed to wander around and learn his surroundings. His day-to-day living becomes difficult due to another dog named Lip-Lip, who is a puppy that is larger than White Fang and is always on the alert to attack him. Lip-Lip also teams up with the other puppies in the camp to go against White Fang and make his life miserable. Later Kiche is released from her leash and allowed to wander the grounds as well. White Fang tries to encourage Kiche to return to the wild and does what he can to lead her away from the Indian camp. He runs out toward the wilderness hoping she will follow, but she always returns back to the camp. His call is stronger to return with his mother rather than go out into the wild alone. Plus, he is still just a cub and is in the process of growing up.

It was at this point that White Fang learns a most difficult and painful lesson. To quote London: **"In the Wild the time of a mother with her young is short; but** under the dominion of man it is sometimes even shorter. Thus it was with White Fang. Gray Beaver was in the debt of Three Eagles. Three Eagles was going away on a trip up the Mackenzie to the Great Slave Lake. A strip of scarlet cloth, a bearskin, twenty cartridges, and Kiche, went to pay the debt. White Fang saw his mother taken aboard Three Eagles' canoe, and tried to follow her. A blow from Three Eagles knocked him backward to the land. The canoe shoved off. He sprang into the water and swam after it, to the sharp cries of Gray Beaver to return. Even a man-animal, a god, White Fang ignored, such was the terror he was in of losing his mother.

But gods are accustomed to being obeyed, and Gray Beaver wrathfully launched a canoe in pursuit. When he overtook White Fang, he reached down and by the nape of the neck lifted him clear of the water. He did not deposit him at once in the bottom of the canoe. Holding him suspended with one hand, with the other hand he proceeded to give him a beating. And it *was* a beating. His hand was heavy. Every blow was shrewd to hurt; and he delivered a multitude of blows.

Impelled by the blows that rained upon him, now from this side, now from that, White Fang swung back and forth like an erratic and jerky pendulum. Varying were the emotions that surged through him. At first, he had known surprise. Then came a momentary fear, when he yelped several times to the impact of the hand. But this was quickly followed by anger. His free nature asserted itself, and he showed his teeth and snarled fearlessly in the face of the wrathful god. This but served to make the god more wrathful. The blows came faster, heavier, more shrewd to hurt.

Gray Beaver continued to beat, White Fang continued to snarl. But this could not last forever. One or the other must give over, and that one was White Fang. Fear surged through him again. For the first time he was being really man-handled. The occasional blows of sticks and stones he had previously experienced were as caresses compared with this. He broke down and began to cry and yelp. For a time each blow brought a yelp from him; but fear passed into terror, until finally his yelps were voiced in unbroken succession, unconnected with the rhythm of the punishment.

At last Gray Beaver withheld his hand. White Fang, hanging limply, continued to cry. This seemed to satisfy his master, who flung him down roughly in the bottom of the canoe. In the meantime the canoe had drifted down the stream. Gray Beaver picked up the paddle. White Fang was in his way. He spurned him savagely with his foot. In that moment White Fang's free nature flashed forth again, and he sank his teeth into the moccasined foot.

The beating that had gone before was as nothing compared with the beating he now received. Gray Beaver's wrath was terrible; likewise was White Fang's fright. Not only the hand, but the hard wooden paddle was used upon him; and he was bruised and sore in all his small body when he was again flung down in the canoe. Again, and this time with purpose, did Gray Beaver kick him. White Fang did not repeat his attack on the foot. He had learned another lesson of his bondage. Never, no matter what the circumstance, must he dare to bite the god who was lord and master over him; the body of the lord and master was sacred, not to be defiled by the teeth of such as he. That was evidently the crime of crimes, the one offense there was no condoning nor overlooking."

Contemplation

This horrible beating by Gray Beaver is difficult to read and a very painful reality for White Fang. Was it really necessary? And if so, for what reason? Did it have to be done to such an extent? Was it the only way? These are all fair questions. We can only speculate but we know Gray Beaver was dealing with an animal that had been raised in the wild and was unpredictable and had been given his name for a reason. He had already bitten humans twice: once in the hand when he was originally caught in the wild and now Gray Beaver in the foot while in the canoe. As to the severity of the beating there was this question Gray Beaver had to ask himself: what does it take for this little cub to obey and be tamed?

For his part, White Fang could ask himself, what did he do wrong? He had been living like he had always lived, according to what he had learned in the wild. He wanted to be with his mother. What is wrong with that? The beating was non-sensical to him. He was simply protecting himself and living by the laws of survival which he knew growing up.

If we look at this beating through a wider lens, however, it may give us a glimpse into something deeper, something which spans the species: i.e. the mystery of suffering. White Fang is abruptly and painfully brought into a much greater reality beyond his comprehension. What he does not know is that Gray Beaver has the desire to teach him something surpassing what he can possibly imagine. The wolf/ wild dog as a natural wildlife creature is a good in and of itself. But it has the potential to ascend and achieve something higher, more advanced. With proper training it can also be useful for human society. Gray Beaver knew the eventual productive role that White Fang could play as he grew up into adulthood including being a sled dog, a guard dog and a companion. But first he needed to learn obedience.

In a similar manner, we humans are like White Fang at times in our relationship with God. For instance, as White Fang cannot understand the punishment he is given by Gray Beaver, we often cannot understand the suffering which we undergo in this life. Suffering seems nonsensical to us just as the beating seemed nonsensical to White Fang. The way we see it, suffering can prevent us from doing that which we want to do – from living the type of life we want to live or from fully enjoying the fulfillment of our desires and wants. And if God is supposed to be a loving God how can He allow us to often go through so much misery? Is that really love?

Yet the picture is much different if we try to allow ourselves to look at it from the other side. As superior as Gray Beaver is in intelligence and power over White Fang, the true God is infinitely more than we humans. Similar to the elevated role that an obedient and tamed animal can have in the company of mankind can be the elevated role that suffering can open in our hearts within the province of God. Suffering is often that which we most avoid and which we most dislike. And yet it is suffering that God often utilizes to stir us from the mundanities of daily life into the deeper realities of our existence. It was utilized to teach White Fang to obey man and to no longer live as he was in the wild, strictly for himself and for survival. Likewise, suffering can be a way to teach us to obey God and to go beyond living just for ourselves and our own wants and needs.

Similar to Gray Beaver's plans for White Fang, God may have further plans for us, plans beyond our own comprehension, plans only He can understand. It is suffering which can jar us to the very core and can humble us in the presence of that which is far greater and far superior. It is suffering that can elevate us in ways we never would have thought, to widen our scope and understanding and challenge us to look at things in a different light. And it is suffering which can be the painful birthing process of a new and higher state of life, a life intertwined more intimately with our God.

Chapter 4

The Ancient Covenant

With Kiche being used to help pay a debt by Gray Beaver, White Fang is now all alone at the camp. He continues to be tortured by the larger puppy, Lip-Lip. With his being part wild, however, he is always able to outrun the other dogs and therefore escape any serious injury. He also becomes quite good at dog fighting, which at times can be quite savage. At times Gray Beaver has to defend White Fang from Lip-Lip and the other dogs with the use of a club. White Fang, thus, obeys Gray Beaver whom he is becoming dependent on and who he views as a god. In the process he learns a new law to follow: **"TO OPPRESS THE WEAK AND OBEY THE STRONG."**

Gray Beaver has a young son by the name of Mitsah, and they are planning a trip in December up the Mackenzie River. In order to carry all of his possessions, Gray Beaver gives to his son a small sled and tells him to have all of the puppies pull it. Thus, White Fang is included in this team of puppies. White Fang eventually becomes the lead dog and because of this becomes a tyrant when dealing with the other dogs.

Later, White Fang learns more about the god's laws of fairness and justice. Mit-sah ends up being unjustly attacked by a group of boys and White Fang leaps among the attackers and scatters them, thus saving Mit-sah from any further injury during the skirmish. For this action, Gray Beaver awards White Fang with an extra ration of fresh meat. From this and other experiences, White Fang learns about the laws of property and when to defend Gray Beaver's property from other gods. As the author notes, **"It was in line with these experiences that White Fang came to learn the law of property and the duty of the defense of property. From the protection of his god's body to the protection of his god's possessions was a step, and this step he made. What was his god's was to be defended against all the world – even to the extent of biting other gods. Not only was such an act sacrilegious in its nature, but it was fraught with peril. The gods were all-powerful and a dog was no match against them; yet White Fang learned to face them, fiercely belligerent and unafraid. Duty rose above fear and thieving gods learned to leave Gray Beaver's property alone…**

The months went by binding stronger and stronger the covenant between dog and man. This was the ancient covenant that the first wolf that came in from the Wild entered into with man. And, like all succeeding wolves and wild dogs that had done likewise, White Fang worked the covenant out for himself. The terms were simple. For the possession of a flesh-and-blood god, he exchanged his own liberty. Food and fire, protection and companionship, were

some of the things he received from the god. In return, he guarded the god's property, defended his body, worked for him, and obeyed him."

Contemplation #1

It is intriguing that the author uses the term "covenant" when describing the relationship between dog and man. He talks about the "ancient covenant" that the first wolf that came in from the wild entered into with man. The use of the term "covenant" reminds us of the Biblical context describing a deep, binding relationship, a family bond. When we think of that ancient covenant we think of the relationship between God and His chosen people, the Israelites.

Whereas the relationship in that context was between God and man, this relationship was between man and dog. It applied to all succeeding wolves and wild dogs that followed that ancient covenant and came in from the wild. The terms as in the above example were noted to be simple. In this case, for the possession of a flesh and blood god, White Fang needed to exchange his own liberty. This was a big undertaking as it meant that he had to give up his prior life in the wild. He needed to give up his prior free and yet savage and more primitive existence. He could no longer do as he pleased but had to live his life within certain laws or limitations that were placed upon him by Gray Beaver. In exchange for this he received certain benefits provided for him by Gray Beaver. Some of the benefits included food and fire, protection and companionship. In exchange for these, however, he did have specific duties which he was supposed to fulfill for Gray Beaver. Those duties included guarding Gray Beaver's property, defending Gray Beaver, working for him, and obeying him. The relationship was that of a covenantal relationship. It was not a type of contract or a mere legally binding agreement, but it was something deeper. It was a becoming a part of Gray Beaver's family. It was an intimate association and reflection of Gray Beaver.

Likewise we can see a mirrored image with that other ancient covenant between God and man. This time, though, it was not just between God and a single person, but between God and a people. It started out back in the very beginning with Adam and Eve and a marital covenant. It then proceeds with Noah and Noah's household with the rainbow exemplifying a familial covenant. It then moves on to the promise made to Abraham and the resultant growth into a tribe of people. As the tribe expands it becomes a nation led by Moses with the Passover as a sign. It then becomes a kingdom under David and later Solomon with the building of the temple. God establishes this covenant and the terms of it also were simple. In exchange for a God, in this case, the one, true God, man must in a similar way exchange some of his own liberty. He is not allowed to live a more primitive, savage, carnal type of existence. The bar has been raised and he must live within certain rules.

For White Fang, who learned the laws of Gray Beaver and of living in concert with Gray Beaver, there were rules to follow. White Fang could not bite his flesh and blood god, nor his family, and he needed to obey his flesh and blood god. Likewise the Israelites were given laws that they needed to follow. The laws were the Ten

Commandments and the teachings by God, through Moses. And like White Fang, who needed to follow the laws of his god Gray Beaver, the Israelites needed to obey and follow the laws of their God, the true God. For his part in the covenant, White Fang received certain benefits. Some of these included food and fire, protection and companionship. Likewise, for their role in the covenant with the true God, the Israelites received certain benefits. These included food, even to the point of miraculously being given manna from heaven. It included fire, the actual fire of God himself over the ark of the covenant as the Israelites wandered through the desert. It included protection with God directly intervening in the conquering of the multiple enemies the Israelites faced as they entered into the promised land and grew from a tribe into a nation and into a kingdom. Lastly, he provided them companionship. It was not a companionship between man and dog, between one limited being and another less superior. It was instead between the Almighty, the All-Knowing with his creature. It was a walking in the garden together with Adam and Eve. It was a calling out directly with very specific instructions for Noah and the ark. It was a reference to the skies as God described to Abraham the myriad descendants he would have. It was the use of fire again as God actually conversed with Moses in the burning bush. And it was the calling out of David as king. Yes, food and fire, protection and companionship. We can see them in both ancient covenants. In return for this, the Jewish people had their own role. For God to give them these benefits, the Jewish people had to do certain things in return. As White Fang was to guard his god's property, defend his body and work for him, so were the Jewish people to guard the ark of the covenant which God had given them, defend His teachings and work for God. As White Fang was to obey Gray Beaver, so were the Jewish people to obey God and the commandments and teachings he gave them.

So we can see the similarities between the ancient covenant of wolf or wild dog and man to that of man and God. There are requirements that need to be fulfilled from both sides. For the lesser party it is a sort of elevation, a calling from a lower to a higher level of existence. Its essence, however, is as a family bond, a deep intimate relationship.

Contemplation #2

The Book of Hebrews gives us a sustained explanation of how the old covenant involving God and the Israelites was a shadow of the new covenant. It indicates how the new covenant is a complete and permanent fulfillment of the old covenant with Christ as the role of mediator between God and humanity. And while we discussed in the contemplation above the similarities between the ancient covenant of wolf or wild dog and man to the ancient covenant of man and God involving the Israelites, we can see a further similarity if we look at it in terms of the new covenant. In the ancient covenant between wolf and wild dog with man, it was man's role to again provide the following: food and fire, protection, and companionship. It was also the role of God in the ancient covenant to provide these to the Israelites as discussed above. In the new covenant, however, it is the role of Christ to provide these to His church. And He does so as follows: He provides us food in the form of the Eucharist, His actual body, His real presence which He first instituted at the Last Supper. He provides us fire with the gift of the Holy Spirit, first coming down amongst the apostles at Pentecost. He provides us companionship, initially in person while He walked the earth, and subsequently in part sacramental and eucharistic, in part written through His word and in part directly through prayer. And He provides us protection against the evil one with the angels and through the church with the word of God, the sacraments He initiated, His teachings and through prayer. The benefit of the new covenant is that Christ provides us Himself as the mediator between God and man.

In exchange for this benefit, however, there are requirements of us. These requirements are similar to the requirements of White Fang in his relationship with Gray Beaver. He needed to guard Gray Beaver's property, defend his body, work for him and obey him. In a likewise manner, as part of the new covenant, it is our role to fulfill this part as well. We are to guard God's property, which in this case means all of the church's teachings and truths. We are to defend His body, which is in reality the church itself since the church is Christ's body on earth. We are to work for Christ by doing what He told us: loving the Lord our God with all our heart, with all our mind and with all our spirit and to love our neighbor as ourselves. And lastly we are to obey Him and to follow His commandments and teachings. It is in the end a type of mutual self-giving. As Christ gives of Himself totally for us, we are to give of ourselves totally for Him.

Chapter 5

The Cage of Horror

The Yukon Gold Rush was in full swing. People were coming from the south up into northern Canada to try to strike it rich. The following summer, Gray Beaver packed up great bundles of furs, mittens, and moccasins and along with White Fang, canoed up to Fort Yukon with his goods to sell. As they arrived, White Fang was further awed at the presence of Fort Yukon and of the men that lived there. He had never seen such a large building before. Gray Beaver then set up shop at Fort Yukon and was able to turn a very healthy profit on all the goods he had brought with him.

White Fang, on the other hand, had time on his hands. Gray Beaver was occupied. There was plenty of food and it was summer. White Fang began amusing himself watching the large boats that arrived regularly bringing in new prospectors. Often the prospectors would bring along their dogs from the southland. White Fang ended up entertaining himself by fighting these dogs that had come up from the south. They were easy prey for a dog of White Fang's experience and initial upbringing in the wild.

One of the few men who lived permanently in Fort Yukon took a devious interest in White Fang, particularly because of his ability to dog fight. This man was nicknamed "Beauty" Smith. Actually, in London's own words, this is a misnomer as this "Beauty" was noted by the author to be **"preeminently ugly"** and even a **"monstrosity."** In addition, his outer appearance was symbolic of his inner nature as he was noted to be **"the weakest of the weak-kneed and sniveling cowards."** Beauty Smith did the cooking for the other men in the Fort, the dishwashing and cleaning. The other men at the Fort did not like him, but basically tolerated him. They also feared him as he would have cowardly rages and they were concerned that he might try to put poison in their coffee or a shot in the back.

White Fang did not like Beauty Smith. As the author indicates: **"This was the man that looked at White Fang, delighted in his ferocious prowess, and desired to possess him. He made overtures to White Fang from the first. White Fang began by ignoring him. Later on, when the overtures became more insistent, White Fang bristled and bared his teeth and backed way. He did not like the man. The feel of him was bad. He sensed the evil in him, and feared the extended hand and the attempts at soft-spoken speech. Because of all this, he hated the man.**

With the simpler creatures, good and bad are things simply understood. The good stands for all things that bring easement and satisfaction and surcease from pain. Therefore, the good is liked. The bad stands for all things that are fraught with discomfort, menace, and hurt, and is hated accordingly. White Fang's feel of Beauty Smith was bad. From the man's distorted body and twisted mind, in occult ways, like mists rising from malarial marshes, came emanations of the unhealth within. Not by reasoning, not by the five senses alone, but by other and remoter and uncharted senses, came the feeling to White Fang that the man was ominous with evil, pregnant with hurtfulness, and therefore a thing bad, and wisely to be hated."

Beauty Smith offered to buy the dog but because Gray Beaver had done so well with all of his selling, he had no need to sell White Fang. "**But Beauty Smith knew the ways of Indians,**" wrote London. He visited Gray Beaver's camp often and hidden under his coat was always a black bottle of whisky. "**Gray Beaver got the thirst**" per the author and things went from bad to worse for him. Gray Beaver ended up squandering his entire profits on alcohol. At that point, Beauty Smith was able to buy White Fang in exchange for whisky.

White Fang did not want to be owned by Beauty Smith and was able to escape several times to go back to Gray Beaver. With each subsequent escape, however, Beauty Smith beat White Fang more and more severely and the last time after a beating White Fang had difficulty walking. Beauty Smith securely chained White Fang such that he could no longer escape. Gray Beaver eventually left Fort Yukon and White Fang was thus solely owned by Beauty Smith.

What proceeded from here is the lowest part of the story. Beauty Smith was a ruthless master, vicious and cruel. He utilized White Fang as a fighting dog and arranged for bets. As White Fang was so successful, Beauty Smith became a dog fight promoter to gain even more income. He kept White Fang in a cage with no other outside activities or life other than the intermittent dog or dogs or lynx or whatever was arranged for White Fang to fight. He purposefully withheld food from White Fang to make him more aggressive. Beauty Smith's cruel treatment of White Fang only made him a more vicious and successful fighter, and the profits continued to go up. Beauty Smith took great delight in White Fang's killing of the other animals presented to him. White Fang invariably won and achieved a reputation in the land. He was noted as **"The Fighting Wolf"** and he was taken in his cage for public viewing like a carnival act.

London notes about White Fang: **"He knew only hate and lost himself in the passion of it. Life had become a hell to him. He had not been made for the close confinement wild beasts endure at the hands of man. And yet it was in precisely in this way that he was treated. Men stared at him, poked sticks between the bars to make him snarl and then laughed at him…**

If Beauty Smith had in him a devil, White Fang had another; and the two of them raged against each other unceasingly. In the days before, White Fang had had the wisdom to cower down and submit to a man with a club in his hand; but this wisdom now left him. The mere sight of Beauty Smith was sufficient to send him into transports of fury. And when they came to close quarters, and he had been beaten back by a club, he went on growling and snarling and showing his fangs. The last growl could never be extracted from

him. No matter how terribly he was beaten, he had always another growl; and when Beauty Smith gave up and withdrew, the defiant growl followed after him, or White Fang sprang at the bars of the cage bellowing his hatred."

At long last, White Fang met his match in a heavily promoted fight against a bulldog named Cherokee. White Fang had never seen a bulldog before and the two of them initially did not want to fight. Later, with coaxing from the bulldog's owner, the fight began. It was a contrast between the quickness of White Fang and the steady determination and machine like jaws of the bulldog. The bulldog's neck was so thick that White Fang could not inflict adequate injury and the bulldog was instead able to close his jaws closer and closer to White Fang's throat. White Fang was in a position of surrender on his back with the bulldog on top of him. The bulldog held on, never loosening, and had a vice-like grip. White Fang was unable to escape the grip and was at the point of death. Knowing that the fight appeared over and with all the money he appeared to have lost, Beauty Smith sprang upon White Fang and began to savagely kick him. Fortunately the story does not end here, but we will pick that up in the next chapter.

Contemplation

Evil exists. We see this loud and clear in the behaviors of Beauty Smith. It is interesting if we look at his evil behavior from the covenantal perspective which we discussed in the last chapter. If you recall, the ancient covenant between wolf or wild dog and man had requirements that needed to be fulfilled from both sides. From the side of mankind, food and fire, protection and companionship were some of the things the dog received. In return the dog guarded the property, defended his owner's body, worked for him and obeyed him. With Beauty Smith, this covenant was cruelly twisted in how it was applied to White Fang. The food was withheld purposefully to make White Fang more hungry and a more vicious dog fighter. With fire, there was only the fire of hatred and angry selfishness in the monstrous eyes of Beauty Smith. There was no warming by the fire as White Fang was instead kept in a chilly cage in the bitter arctic cold. As far as protection, this did not occur and in fact the opposite occurred. Beauty Smith's whole focus was to put White Fang at risk for profit with each and every fight. And companionship was simply non-existent. White Fang was kept in complete isolation. He was trapped and miserable. Beauty Smith's abuse is the antithesis of a covenantal relationship.

Likewise, White Fang ended up responding in a similar manner and while Beauty Smith did not fulfill his part of the covenantal relationship, neither did White Fang. He did not guard Beauty Smith's property and loathed anything having to do with Beauty Smith. He did not defend Beauty Smith's body and in fact did quite the opposite. He attacked Beauty Smith at any chance he could. He did not work for Beauty Smith, but only was forced to do the dog fighting because he had no other choice. And lastly, he did not obey Beauty Smith. Even when Beauty Smith would beat him, he would growl in defiance or lunge after him with whatever he had left..

The opposite of the covenantal relationship is abuse. And what is interesting is that in this case there was a taking on of each other's characteristics during the process. As vicious as Beauty Smith was to White Fang, White Fang became just as vicious right back. The author notes, **"If Beauty Smith had in him a devil, White Fang had another and the two of them raged against each other, unceasingly"**. *While the author London may or may not have meant the use of the term "devil" as a matter of speech, we nevertheless do need to recognize that the devil himself is indeed real. We cannot believe in Christ without also recognizing and believing in the existence of the devil. For Christ referenced the devil multiple times and dealt with him throughout the time of His public ministry. He dealt with temptation Himself while in the desert prior to beginning His public ministry. He called Peter a devil at one point. In the parable of the sower, He called the devil the enemy. And He exorcised multiple devils on various occasions including in the Gerasene's when He, interestingly enough, sent them into pigs. No, the devil exists and we in our modern society need to, as Christ did, recognize this as a reality.*

Chapter 6

The Love Begins

In the last chapter, we left White Fang seriously losing and near the point of death in the dog fight. A group of men were surrounding the fight and either cheering or jeering (depending on their bets). The bulldog had his jaws clamped on White Fang's throat. White Fang was laying on his back in a position of surrender with the bulldog over him and ever tightening his grip. Fortunately for White Fang, a newcomer shows up at the last minute.

The author tells us: **"In the meantime, the abysmal brute in Beauty Smith had been rising up into his brain and mastering the small bit of sanity that he possessed at best. When he saw White Fang's eyes beginning to glaze, he knew beyond doubt that the fight was lost. Then he broke loose. He sprang upon White Fang and began savagely to kick him. There were hisses from the crowd and cries of protest, but that was all. While this went on, and Beauty Smith continued to kick White Fang, there was a commotion** in the crowd. The tall young newcomer was forcing his way through, shouldering men right and left without ceremony or gentleness. When he broke through into the ring, Beauty Smith was just in the act of delivering another kick. All his weight was on one foot, and he was in a state of unstable equilibrium. At that moment, the newcomer's fist landed a smashing blow full in his face. Beauty Smith's remaining leg left the ground, and his whole body seemed to lift into the air as he turned over backward and struck the snow. The newcomer turned upon the crowd.

'You cowards!' he cried. 'You beasts!'

He was in a rage himself – a sane rage. His gray eyes seemed metallic and steel-like as they flashed upon the crowd. Beauty Smith regained his feet and came toward him, sniffling and cowardly. The newcomer did not understand. He did not know how abject a coward the other was, and thought he was coming back intent on fighting. So, with a 'You beast!' he smashed Beauty Smith over backward with a second blow in the face. Beauty Smith decided that the snow was the safest place for him, and he lay where he had fallen, making no effort to get up."

The newcomer was named Weedon Scott and with his employee, Matt, a dog musher, they began working on extricating the bulldog's jaws from the neck of White Fang. The crowd quieted and began dispersing as betting on arranged dog fights is illegal and the crowd assumed that these two men were associated somehow with the civil authorities. Slowly, painfully, the bulldog's jaw was forcibly opened and White Fang's mangled neck extricated. White Fang was too weak to get up, his eyes were half closed and they were glassy. His tongue protruded. The author tells us:

"To all appearances he looked like a dog that had been strangled to death. Matt examined him.

'Just about all in,' he announced; 'but he's breathin' all right.'

Beauty Smith had regained his feet and come over to look at White Fang.

'Matt, how much is a good sled-dog worth?' Scott asked.

The dog-musher, still on his knees and stooped over White Fang, calculated for a moment.

'Three hundred dollars,' he answered.

'And how much for one that's all chewed up like this one?' Scott asked, nudging White Fang with his foot.

'Half of that,' was the dog-musher's judgment.

Scott turned upon Beauty Smith.

'Did you hear, Mr. Beast? I'm going to take your dog from you, and I'm going to give you a hundred and fifty for him.'

He opened his pocket-book and counted out the bills.

Beauty Smith put his hands behind his back, refusing to touch the proffered money.

'I ain't a-sellin',' he said.

'Oh, yes you are,' the other assured him. 'Because I'm buying. Here's your money. The dog's mine.'

Beauty Smith, his hands still behind him, began to back away.

Scott sprang toward him, drawing his fist back to strike. Beauty Smith cowered down in anticipation of the blow.

'I've got my rights,' he whimpered.

'You've forfeited your rights to own that dog,' was the rejoinder. 'Are you going to take the money? Or do I have to hit you again?'

'All right,' Beauty Smith spoke up with the alacrity of fear. 'But I take the money under protest,' he added. 'The dog's a mint. I ain't a-goin' to be robbed. A man's got his rights.'

'Correct,' Scott answered, passing the money over to him. 'A man's got his rights. But you're not a man. You're a beast.'

'Wait till I get back to Dawson,' Beauty Smith threatened. 'I'll have the law on you.'

'If you open your mouth when you get back to Dawson, I'll have you run out of town. Understand?'

Beauty Smith replied with a grunt.

'Understand?' the other thundered with abrupt fierceness.

'Yes,' Beauty Smith grunted, shrinking away.

'Yes what?'

'Yes sir,' Beauty Smith snarled."

Weedon Scott was a known mining expert working as a consultant from California. He was well connected with the local officials and the gold commissioner was noted to be a friend of his.

White Fang survived the fight and gradually healed.

Thus begins the long process of trying to re-tame White Fang. He had been mistreated for so long that he would become bristling, snarling and ferocious with anyone that came close to him. When Weedon Scott and Matt looked closer, they could see that he had marks across his chest which indicated that he had been a sled dog in the past and had thus been tamed before. They felt that he would be a fine sled dog again if only this could be achieved. Unfortunately, the process proved to be very difficult. After White Fang bit Matt's leg as well as biting Weedon Scott's hand they actually thought about abandoning the project and shooting him as he was basically a menace. They finally decided as a last resort that they would try to show him some consistent kindness to see if that would help with all of his maltreatment.

So Weedon Scott would sit down several feet away from White Fang so that White Fang knew that there was no danger. He had no club, whip or firearm and White Fang was set free. There was no chain around and he was not collared. Scott talked to him in calm, kind words. These were words expressing emotion and gentleness that White Fang had never heard before. He would then toss some meat on the snow at White Fang's feet. This went on multiple times. There came a time when he didn't toss it. The time finally came when he decided to eat the meat from his hand. No punishment came to him. On and on came the kindness and the soothing talk as the sessions continued. Somewhere deep inside White Fang he was moved. Eventually Scott was able to start slowly petting White Fang. This was hard for White Fang and went against everything known to him. He learned to trust this man-animal, however, this god that was caring for him in a way that none of his other masters had. As London tells us: **"But the god talked on softly, and ever the hand rose and fell with non-hostile pats.**

White Fang experienced dual feelings. It was distasteful to his instinct. It restrained him, opposed the will of him toward personal liberty. And yet it was not physically painful. On the contrary, it was even pleasant, in a physical way. The patting movement slowly and carefully changed to a rubbing of the ears about their bases, and the physical pleasure even increased a little. Yet he continued to fear, and he stood on guard, expectant of unguessed evil, alternately suffering and enjoying as one feeling or the other came uppermost and swayed him…"

"It was the beginning of the end for White Fang – the ending of the old life and the reign of hate. A new and incomprehensively fairer life was dawning. It required much thinking and endless patience on the part of Weedon Scott to accomplish this and on the part of White Fang it required nothing less than a revolution…"

"He had gone to the roots of White Fang's nature and with kindness touched to life potencies that had languished and well-nigh perished…"

"Weedon Scott had set himself the task of redeeming White Fang – or rather, of redeeming mankind from the wrong it had done White Fang. It was a matter of principle and conscience. He felt that the ill done White Fang was a debt incurred by man and that it must be paid. So he went out of his way to be especially kind to the Fighting Wolf. Each day he made it a point to caress and pet White Fang, and to do it at length."

This took place over time. White Fang liked this new god. Life was so much better than being in the cage of Beauty Smith. He began being the guard dog of

Weedon Scott's property, similarly to what he had done with Gray Beaver. He looked forward to his caresses. To quote London: **"White Fang was in the process of finding himself. In spite of the maturity of his years and of the savage rigidity of the mold that had formed him, his nature was undergoing an expansion. There was a burgeoning within him of strange feelings and unwonted impulses. His old code of conduct was changing. In the past he had liked comfort and surcease from pain, disliked discomfort and pain, and he had adjusted his actions accordingly. But now it was different. Because of this new feeling within him, he ofttimes elected discomfort and pain for the sake of his god. Thus, in the early morning, instead of roaming and foraging, or lying in a sheltered nook, he would wait for hours on the cheerless cabin-stoop for a sight of the god's face. At night, when the god returned home, White Fang would leave the warm sleeping place he had burrowed in the snow in order to receive the friendly snap of fingers and the word of greeting. Meat, even meat itself, he would forego to be with his god, to receive a caress from him or to accompany him down into the town…"**

"*Like* had been replaced by *love*. And love was the plummet dropped down into the deeps of him where like had never gone. And responsive, out of his deeps had come a new thing – love. That which was given unto him did he return. This was a god indeed, a love-god, a warm and radiant god in whose light White Fang's nature expanded as a flower expands under the sun…"

David G. Smithson, MD

Contemplation #1

In this chapter we can see Weedon Scott as a type for Christ. Both Christ and Weedon Scott carried out acts of expiation, paying a debt, righting a wrong caused by mankind's sin. They both sacrificed themselves with Jesus literally sacrificing himself on the cross while Weedon Scott, instead, sacrificed with his time and concerted effort. He **"made it a point to caress and pet White Fang and to do it at length."** *The goal of both, Christ and Weedon Scott, was to restore those in a fallen state (mankind in the case of Christ, White Fang in the case of Weedon Scott) back to an elevated level of existence. Sacrifice had to be made to accomplish this. It was not something mankind or White Fang respectively could do on their own. Both of them were symbolically 'stuck in the mud' and unable to get out. Mankind in his sinful, fallen state after Adam was kicked out of the Garden, and White Fang with his vicious and menacing demeanor may actually have lowered his state even below that of a wolf or wild dog who was simply trying to survive. It required the directed loving intervention of one superior in existence to come down to the lower level and make it happen, to symbolically bring them up out of the mud.*

As God once walked with Adam, so can we walk with our dogs both literally and figuratively. Both Christ and Weedon Scott were expiating for mankind's sin to once again achieve the point of walking together in an elevated state. Christ with his suffering and death overcame sin and opened the door for mankind to again walk with God in Heaven. Weedon Scott, in a different manner, also overcame death due to sin. This time the death that was overcome potentially involved White Fang as he was so vicious due to the abuse and sin of Beauty Smith. Weedon Scott overcame this with his patience and the sacrifice of his time and attention. Thus, both mankind and White Fang underwent the process of being saved. Mankind, through Christ's intervention as the new Adam, and White Fang, through Weedon Scott's personal intervention.

Let's take a look at a very basic hierarchy of intelligence which can help further illustrate these points. Please see the diagram as noted:

Basic Hierarchy of Intelligence

God

Angels/Demons (fallen angels)

Human Beings

Animal Kingdom

We see God in his omniscience, who is, of course, at the top as the highest intelligence of all. Next in line are the angels. This includes both the good angels and the fallen angels (or demons). Below the angels and demons are human beings and below human beings is the animal kingdom. In looking at this diagram we can see that mankind initially had an elevated position walking with God. With his sin, however, he had the falling out which placed him below the supernatural beings but at the top of the natural world. It is by Christ coming down from above and actually entering into the human experience personally that He undertakes expiation or vicarious suffering in our place to again restore us to the point of being able to once again walk with God in Heaven. He destroyed the finality of death and reopened eternal existence to again be with God.

In a likewise manner, White Fang had a falling out from mankind and thus suffered from a fallen state. He had been walking with mankind which included walking in a covenantal relationship which was functional and mutually satisfying involving Gray Beaver. Unfortunately, with the abusiveness of Beauty Smith, White Fang's demeanor changed such that he could potentially be considered in a state even below his prior natural state in the wild. He was so vicious that there was consideration for actually having to put him to death because he was a potential menace to society. Again, it was by Weedon Scott from an elevated level as a human being reaching down personally and sacrificing of himself in expiating for the sin which had been committed which allowed White Fang to elevate to the higher level to again be walking with mankind.

So we can see a type of mirroring of the process of redemption between both God and man and man and dog. In fact, it was the author London who referred to Weedon Scott as a redeemer of sorts: **"Weedon Scott had set himself the task of redeeming White Fang – or rather of redeeming mankind from the wrong it had done White Fang."** *It was the act of redemption undertaken by Weedon Scott in saving White Fang that is analogous to the method of redemption which Christ has undertaken in saving mankind. Of course, there are some major differences between man and dog with man having free will* and being able to personally choose between good and evil. There is also the fact that mankind was made in God's image and thus could have an even closer, more intimate relationship with God in elevating from the fallen state. But even with those significant differences, there are still certain unique bonding characteristics between man and dog that have been noted (8).

So why did God choose this method of redemption? Why did Christ need to come to earth and become one of us in order to expiate for our sins? How is it that we can see a mirroring of this in the relationship between man and dog? And why does it always involve suffering and/or self-sacrifice? In ways difficult for us to understand, God utilizes suffering as His means for spiritual growth. It is this suffering that is utilized in the redemption process. And while Weedon Scott gave of himself, sacrificed of his time and energies to devote to White Fang's redemption, so did Christ give of Himself to devote to our redemption. To understand Christ better, however, we need to look beyond just an individual basis to the whole human race. Adam's sin was a debasement for all mankind. And we as mankind could not figuratively get out of this mud ourselves. We needed someone from above to come down, rescue us and lift us up out of it. Christ does this as the Son of God and the Son of Man – a representation of all mankind. As Adam's sin affected the whole human race in a fallen state, so does Christ's redemption lift us up to our proper place.

David G. Smithson, MD

Contemplation #2

Inherent in the gift of faith is the role of mystery. If everything were all cold, hard fact there would be no need for faith and thus no role for mystery. However, since faith involves that which is beyond our comprehension then mystery is simply a part of faith. And as mystery exists for man in trying to understand the ways of God so would mystery exist for a dog in trying to understand the ways of man. If I had my golden retriever come into my study and I showed her the map of Canada and where the Yukon is located, she would have absolutely no concept of what I was describing. Our intelligence is so advanced above the canine world that it would be a complete mystery in her mind. Likewise, and even more so, is God advanced over mankind. He is infinitely more advanced than we are. So, it only makes sense that there are mysteries present in our faith..

At one point in my life it used to bother me that there was such mystery, thinking that we humans should, with our superior intellects and scientific know-how, figure out all the answers to these mysteries. I was not alone. That is a common thinking nowadays; to replace God with science. In doing this, however, we are forgetting where we are on the basic hierarchy of intelligence. We must remember that as mankind we are below the supernatural world and at the top of the natural world. It has often been said that there is nothing more complex in the entire universe than the human brain. God ordered all things in the natural world by measure, number and weight and gave us the cognitive abilities to assess these things and to utilize this information. And in doing so, subsequent scientific discoveries have been immensely helpful for mankind. But the supernatural world again is above the natural world. We end up using that which in actuality is below us to try to explain many of the ultimate mysteries that in reality involve God who is infinitely superior to us. We just need to keep our ideas regarding the role of science within its proper context.

In addition, we need to keep our sense of awe, of amazement, as was described by Albert Einstein and Sir Isaac Newton with their quotes in chapter 2. In the end, when it comes to the question of mystery, the answer brings us back to the book of Job. And while the context of Job can help explain why there is suffering in the world, the answer goes beyond just that question. It really involves all of those unanswerable mysteries of our faith. The answer is that God and His ways are simply beyond our comprehension. It is a humbling that we must undergo on our way to giving glory to our God who is infinitely above us.

Contemplation #3

White Fang was open to Weedon Scott's promptings. He was receptive to the outpouring of affection and gradually allowed Weedon Scott to feed him out of his hand and eventually to pet him and thus warmed more and more to him. **"That which was given unto him did he return."** *The affection that was given to White Fang by Weedon Scott was returned and the like turned to love and White Fang's nature blossomed as noted above. If White Fang refused or rebelled along the way the end results may have been very different. In a likewise manner,* *we must be open to God's prompting for ourselves to gradually grow in love of Him. If we are closed to God or rebel, the results may be very different for us as well. Nevertheless, God respects our free will. It is up to us to respond to God's ways, to allow ourselves to grow closer and give of ourselves over to God as White Fang was in the process of giving himself over to Weedon Scott.*

Although Weedon Scott and Matt strongly considered shooting White Fang with his terribly vicious nature, they decided to give him a chance. They saw potential in him. In a similar manner, God will continue to see potential in us. As long as there is still a breath of life, God can and will always give us another chance. It is up to us. It is a type of rebirth but we must be open to it. We must be willing to take the chances and make the changes. It can be a new start, a wonderful new journey into the expanse of God's love.

Chapter 7

The Dark Night

"In the late spring a great trouble came to White Fang. Without warning, the love-master disappeared. There had been warning, but White Fang was unversed in such things and did not understand the packing of a grip. He remembered afterward that this packing had preceded the master's disappearance; but at the time he suspected nothing. That night he waited for the master to return. At midnight the chill wind that blew drove him to shelter at the rear of the cabin. There he drowsed, only half asleep, his ears keyed for the first sound of the familiar step. But, at two in the morning, his anxiety drove him out to the cold front stoop, where he crouched and waited.

But no master came. In the morning the door opened and Matt stepped outside. White Fang gazed at him wistfully. There was no common speech by which he might learn what he wanted to know. The days came and went, but never the master. White Fang, who had never known sickness in his life, became sick. He became very sick, so sick that Matt was finally compelled to bring him inside the cabin. Also, in writing to his employer, Matt devoted a postscript to White Fang.

Weedon Scott reading the letter down in Circle City, came upon the following:

'That dam wolf wont work. Wont eat. Aint got no spunk left. All the dogs is licking him. Wants to know what has become of you, and I don't know how to tell him. Mebbe he is going to die.'

It was as Matt had said. White Fang had ceased eating, lost heart, and allowed every dog of the team to thrash him. In the cabin he lay on the floor near the stove without interest in food, in Matt, nor in life. Matt might talk gently to him or swear at him, it was all the same; he never did more than turn his dull eyes upon the man, then drop his head back to its customary position on his fore-paws.

And then, one night, Matt, reading to himself with moving lips and mumbled sounds, was startled by a low whine from White Fang. He had got upon his feet, his ears cocked toward the door, and he was listening intently. A moment later, Matt heard a footstep. The door opened, and Weedon Scott stepped in. The two men shook hands. Then Scott looked around the room.

'Where's the wolf?' he asked.

Then he discovered him, standing where he had been lying, near to the stove. He had not rushed forward after the manner of other dogs. He stood, watching and waiting.

'Holy smoke!' Matt exclaimed. 'Look at 'm wag his tail!'

Weeden Scott strode half across the room toward him, at the same time calling him. White Fang came to him, not with a great bound, yet quickly. He was awkward from self-consciousness, but as he drew near, his eyes took on a strange expression. Something, an incommunicable vastness of feeling, rose up into his eyes as a light and shone forth.

'He never looked at me that way all the time you was gone,' Matt commented.

Weedon Scott did not hear. He was squatting down on his heels, face to face with White Fang and petting him – rubbing at the roots of the ears, making long, caressing strokes down the neck to the shoulders, tapping the spine gently with the balls of his fingers. And White Fang was growling responsively, the crooning note of the growl more pronounced than ever.

But that was not all. What of his joy, the great love in him, ever surging and struggling to express itself, succeeded in finding a new mode of expression. He suddenly thrust his head forward and nudged his way in between the master's arms and body. And here, confined, hidden from view of all except his ears, no longer growling, he continued to nudge and snuggle.

The two men looked at each other. Scott's eyes were shining.

'Gosh!' said Matt in an awe-stricken voice.

A moment later, when he had recovered himself, he said, 'I always insisted that wolf was a dog. Look at 'm!'

With the return of the love-master, White Fang's recovery was rapid...

Having learned to snuggle, White Fang was guilty of it often. It was the final word. He could not go beyond it. The one thing of which he had always been particularly jealous, was his head. He had always disliked to have it touched. It was the Wild in him, the fear of hurt and of the trap, that had given rise to the panicky impulses to avoid contacts. It was the mandate of his instinct that that head must be free. And now, with the love-master, his snuggling was the deliberate act of putting himself into a position of hopeless helplessness. It was an expression of perfect confidence, of absolute self-surrender, as though he said: 'I put myself into thy hands. Work thou thy will with me.'"

Contemplation #1

When Mother Teresa of Calcutta was a young nun, she received a second calling to reach out specifically to the poorest of the poor. After receiving approval, she began a new order, the Missionaries of Charity. She then spent the rest of her life caring for those for whom no one else cared, those desolate and forgotten souls. She cared for their physical and spiritual needs; dressing their wounds, feeding them, trying to ease their pain, comforting them. Many other women joined her in this selfless, sacrificial life. And yet, throughout much of the rest of her life, we found out after her death that she had felt an ongoing spiritual dryness. She did not feel close to God with her regular prayer life. She often felt abandoned, *isolated, alone. She herself called it "the darkness" and her writings indicated it lasted roughly 50 years. She wrote that her smile was actually masking a multitude of pains and that she often felt unwanted and unloved by God. It was an intense inner suffering. Yet outwardly it was hidden.. And Mother Teresa, now Saint Teresa of Calcutta, is not alone. When we look at the lives of many other saints, they also suffered from this same occurrence. In the 16th century, Saint John of the Cross described it as "the dark night of the soul." Why would God allow such suffering? What is the purpose of it?*

Since leaving Beauty Smith, White Fang's relationship with Weedon Scott had grown strong. Like had grown into love. Weedon Scott went out of his way to show affection to White Fang and that which was given unto him did he return. White Fang's nature was expanding as he was growing in his affection for Weedon Scott. But then, one day, unbeknownst to White Fang, Weedon Scott suddenly left. It was beyond White Fang's comprehension as to why Weedon Scott left. White Fang felt abandoned, isolated. He had this growing love and intense change that was going on all about him and now it had stopped. He became sick. He couldn't eat. He lost interest in other things. It was in essence an intense suffering that White Fang was undergoing and he knew not why. But once Weedon Scott reappeared after the long absence, White Fang's love grew even more. He found a new mode of expression, snuggling himself between his master's arms and body. This was an expression of an even deeper love than had existed prior to Weedon Scott's absence. And Weedon Scott responded likewise with eyes shining and an even deeper outward expression of emotion.

God often utilizes suffering as a means for greater spiritual growth. He will allow it for a greater and deeper love for Him and with Him. We can see the results of what happened with White Fang; the subsequent deepening of the relationship, the increased intimacy expressed in a way never done before. And in a likewise manner, we can see how God may utilize this same approach with us as exemplified by many of the saints.

Regarding this new means of snuggling as a deeper expression of love the author notes: **"It was an expression of perfect confidence, of self-surrender, as though he said : "I put myself into thy hands, work thou thy will with me' "**. *I find it amazing that the author put a direct quotation which referenced Christ when talking about this self-surrender of White Fang. Nevertheless, as White Fang surrendered himself to Weedon Scott, and Christ surrendered Himself to His Father, are we like the saints to surrender ourselves to our God.*

Contemplation #2

Note: this will be a different type of contemplation from all of those previous. It is instead more of a meditation or pondering. It is an analogy of White Fang's "dark night" of separation from Weedon Scott followed by Weedon Scott's emotional response upon returning (at the very end of this contemplation remember the glance shared between Weedon Scott and Matt). It will be divided into two different sections. Please imagine with me…

A Glimpse Back in Time: As the evening wore on, she was at last alone to her own thoughts. She again slumped to her knees, the tears continuing to fall. The sights and sounds of the day were surrounding her. What a horrible, horrible day. Her arms reached out and her face looked upward. What utter agony He had gone through. Blood streaming down His face. Painfully gasping for the next breath. Each second was like an eternity. She felt so helpless looking up at Him. She tried to blot out the jeers and sarcastic comments of the crowds all around. She kept her eyes intently on Him. Oh, if only she could hold Him, comfort Him, ease His pain. But no. It wasn't to be. On and on it went. When it was finally over, He was taken down. Utterly lifeless, He was laid out on her lap. Her empty arms assumed the same position of earlier in the day, going through the same motions, caressing Him, stroking His hair, kissing His face, reliving the excruciating pain. My Son is dead! My Son! My Son! A fresh, new gush of tears streamed down her face…

Her thoughts traveled back in time. She remembered His birth. In a stable of all places and she would rest Him in a manger! The tears stopped for a while as she smiled. How wonderful and patient Joseph was. She relived holding her tiny little newborn Son. So beautiful. So tender. What a miracle! She then remembered she and Joseph taking Him to the Temple for His presentation. Yes, there were the turtle doves that were given over. And afterwards this older man comes up to them. Right out of the blue. Simeon was his name. And the incredible things he said about her Son. Her tiny, baby Son, sleeping so peacefully in her arms. This older man was saying amazing things about Him. What did it all mean? How did he know this? And then the comment regarding her. Yes. It wasn't just about Jesus. It was also about her. He talked about a sword that would pierce her heart. A sword! And not just for Him, but for her! Of course! Of course! The tears started back up. She could feel that sword. This is what he meant! She could feel it right now! The day's events flooded back. She could feel that sword so deep, so piercing. Her Son was dead! Her Son! Jesus! Her lovely Jesus! She felt the deep intense agony all over again. Deeper and deeper it bore. Floods of tears gushed forth. It continued on and on... Oh, it was a dark night indeed, a very, very dark night.

A Glimpse Later in Time – As He sat on His throne, His risen body was absolutely glowing. His smile was compelling. His eyes lovingly met His Father's eyes. All heaven was assembled. The Saints were all there, dressed in their beautiful white robes, and the choirs of angels were surrounding, singing an unbelievably magnificent chorus. The stage was set, the time had arrived. Attended to by the cherubim, her entrance was announced. She was coming! The excitement was palpable. There she is! How incredibly beautiful she is!. Her blue mantel was draped over her. She scanned the crowd as a great roar rose from amongst them. It was the coronation, the crowning of the Queen! What a stupendous event!

God the Father gazed at this lovely creature that stood before Him. She had always given Him her fiat. Her "yes" was consistent and true. No one had ever been like her and no one will ever be like her. She was the mother of His Son, spouse of the Holy Spirit and His own daughter. His eyes focused again on His Son. The two looked at each other. The Father's eyes were shining.

Chapter 8

Enemy Combat

While the previously noted relationship between White Fang and Weedon Scott was ever deepening, White Fang was also being put to good use as a sled dog and as a guard dog. The author describes his learning process as a guard dog as the story continues: **"And so, because he needed a god and because he preferred Weedon Scott to Beauty Smith, White Fang remained. In acknowledgment of fealty, he proceeded to take upon himself the guardianship of his master's property. He prowled about the cabin while the sled-dogs slept, and the first night-visitor to the cabin fought him off with a club until Weedon Scott came to the rescue. But White Fang soon learned to differentiate between thieves and honest men, to appraise the true value of step and carriage. The man who travelled, loud-stepping, the direct line to the cabin door, he let alone – though he watched him vigilantly until the door opened and he received the indorsement of the master. But the man who went softly, by circuitous** ways, peering with caution, seeking after secrecy – that was the man who received no suspension of judgment from White Fang, and who went away abruptly, hurriedly, and without dignity..."

"One night, not long after the return, Scott and Matt sat at a game of cribbage preliminary to going to bed. 'Fifteen-two, fifteen-four an' a pair makes six,' Matt was pegging up, when there was an outcry and sound of snarling without. They looked at each other as they started to rise to their feet.

'The wolf's nailed somebody," Matt said.

A wild scream of fear and anguish hastened them.

'Bring a light!' Scott shouted, as he sprang outside.

Matt followed with the lamp, and by its light they saw a man lying on his back in the snow. His arms were folded, one above the other, across his face and throat. Thus he was trying to shield himself from White Fang's teeth. And there was need for it. White Fang was in a rage, wickedly making his attack on the most vulnerable spot. From shoulder to wrist of the crossed arms, the coat-sleeve, blue flannel shirt and undershirt were ripped in rags, while the arms themselves were terribly slashed and streaming blood.

All this the two men saw in the first instant. The next instant Weedon Scott had White Fang by the throat and was dragging him clear. White Fang struggled and snarled, but made no attempt to bite, while he quickly quieted down at a sharp word from the master.

Matt helped the man to his feet. As he arose he lowered his crossed arms, exposing the bestial face of

Beauty Smith. The dog-musher let go of him precipitately, with action similar to that of a man who has picked up live fire. Beauty Smith blinked in the lamplight and looked about him. He caught sight of White Fang and terror rushed into his face.

At the same moment Matt noticed two objects lying in the snow. He held his lamp close to them, indicating them with his toe for his employer's benefit – a steel dog-chain and a stout club.

Weedon Scott saw and nodded. Not a word was spoken. The dog-musher laid his hand on Beauty Smith's shoulder and faced him to the right about. No word needed to be spoken. Beauty Smith started.

In the meantime the love-master was patting White Fang and talking to him.

'Tried to steal you, eh? And you wouldn't have it! Well, well, he made a mistake, didn't he?'

'Must 'a' thought he had hold of seventeen devils', the dog musher sniggered.

White Fang, still wrought up and bristling, growled and growled, the hair slowly lying down, the crooning note remote and dim, but growing in his throat."

Contemplation

What happened to White Fang in this attack by Beauty Smith is analogous to what can happen to us from a spiritual perspective. White Fang was previously under the chains of Beauty Smith – he literally was caged and terribly abused. He was subsequently freed by Weedon Scott. He was growing in his love for Weedon Scott, blooming and becoming a new creation. But Beauty Smith didn't forget about White Fang. No, he was scheming, devising his devious plan to steal away White Fang. As a human being he was obviously much more intelligent and could utilize various devices or techniques in attempting to complete his evil plan. He could also arrange to strike at any time. He could look for a time when White Fang was particularly vulnerable. And while White Fang did savagely attack Beauty Smith, it was Weedon Scott and Matt that ended up protecting White Fang and sent Beauty Smith on his way.

The spiritual world tends to operate in a similar manner. We are all involved in a spiritual battle whether we know it or not. This becomes particularly apparent when one leaves the chains and bondage of sin and starts to grow closer to God, as White Fang was growing closer to Weedon Scott. Like Beauty Smith, the devil does not forget. He will scheme, devising his own devious plan to try to steal the person away from God and put him or her back under the bondage of sin. And similar to the superior intelligence of a human over a dog is this superior intelligence of the evil one over mankind. He can utilize various devices or techniques in attempting to complete his plan. He can also arrange to strike at any time. He may look for a time when the person is particularly vulnerable. And since this is a battle between superior forces, it behooves the sought after soul to call upon similar forces in the battle. Saint Paul indicated that our battle is not against flesh and blood, but against principalities and powers. As an Archangel, Saint Michael is often utilized as a powerful saint to call upon in this context. And the name of Jesus is noted to be particularly powerful in and of itself. Entire books have been written about the immense power of Jesus' name alone within the spiritual realm.

As there was a battle for White Fang as he moved from the side of evil to the side of good, there is also a likewise battle for each one of us. As White Fang was more vulnerable alone, so are we more vulnerable alone. We must stay close to God and call on Him and His angels for our ongoing protection. The spiritual battle rages on. It happened to our Lord. It happened to the saints. Don't think that we will be spared.

Chapter 9

A New Land

It was time for Weedon Scott to leave the Yukon and to return permanently to his extended family home in California. As the time was coming near for him to depart, he and Matt would sometimes have long discussions in their cabin about what to do with White Fang. Having been raised in the frigid, savage Yukon wild, Weedon Scott knew he needed to leave him to stay with Matt. But it was difficult as they had grown so attached.

As the day of his departure grew near, White Fang detected things changing around the cabin. He had a sense of what was coming. On the actual day of his departure, Weedon Scott and Matt decided to call White Fang into the cabin and then locked him in. They then proceeded to go down to the steamboat that Weedon Scott was to take back to California. Alone, locked in the cabin with the master and all of his belongings gone, White Fang sadly let out a long wolf howl, crying to the sky with his woes.

Meanwhile, Weedon Scott and Matt were on the steamboat plank, getting ready for the boarding onto the ship. The next thing they saw was a cut-up and gouged White Fang close to them! In their shock and dismay they realized White Fang had jumped through the window of the cabin in order to try to get back together with his master. Moved by compassion, Weedon Scott then decided to try to take White Fang along in returning back to his home in California.

When they landed in San Francisco, the city with all its' noises, monstrous cable and electric cars, automobiles and many people were quite a site to White Fang. To him it was a magnificent show of power and awe. They then traveled to Weeden Scott's home, named Sierra Vista, which included a large house and an extended tract of land. There were hay fields and hills and pastures. As they unloaded, White Fang was to meet the two other family dogs that already lived on the property. One was a female sheepdog named Collie who was barking and challenging him from the start. The other was a deer hound named Dick that White Fang simply needed to get along with. There were many people living on the estate that White Fang needed to consider as well. In the Scott extended family this included Weedon Scott's parents, Judge Scott and his wife, as well as Weedon Scott's two adult sisters Beth and Mary, along with his wife Alice and their two young children. As White Fang learned all this, he learned what was of value to his master. Thus, what was dear to his master was cherished by White Fang and guarded carefully. White Fang also needed to differentiate between the members of the family and the servants of the household. Outside of the household there was even more for White Fang to learn. The master's domain was a large property and complex, yet it did have its boundaries. There was a country road and there were fences and he learned that the other side of the fences were the particular domain of other human gods.

As the author notes: **"A myriad laws governed all these things and determined conduct; yet he did not know the speech of the gods, nor was there any way for him to learn save by experience. He obeyed his natural impulses until they ran him counter to some law. When this had been done a few times, he learned the law and after that observed it.**

But most potent in his education were the cuff of the master's hand, the censure of the master's voice. Because of White Fang's very great love, a cuff from the master hurt him far more than any beating Gray Beaver or Beauty Smith had ever given him. They had hurt only the flesh of him; beneath the flesh the spirit had still raged, splendid and invincible. But with the master the cuff was always too light to hurt the flesh. Yet it went deeper. It was an expression of the master's disapproval, and White Fang's spirit wilted under it.

In point of fact, the cuff was rarely administered. The master's voice was sufficient. By it White Fang knew whether he did right or not. By it he trimmed his conduct and adjusted his actions. It was the compass by which he steered and learned to chart the manners of a new land and life.

In the Northland, the only domesticated animal was the dog. All other animals lived in the Wild, and were, when not too formidable, lawful spoil for any dog. All his days White Fang had foraged among the

The Parable of White Fang

live things for food. It did not enter his head that in the Southland it was otherwise. But this he was to learn early in his residence in Santa Clara Valley. Sauntering around the corner of the house in the early morning, he came upon a chicken that had escaped from the chicken-yard. White Fang's natural impulse was to eat it. A couple of bounds, a flash of teeth and a frightened squawk, and he had scooped in the adventurous fowl. It was farm-bred and fat and tender; and White Fang licked his chops and decided that such fare was good.

Later in the day, he chanced upon another stray chicken near the stables…"

"'He'll learn to leave the chickens alone,' the master said. 'But I can't give him the lesson until I catch him in the act.'

Two nights later came the act, but on a more generous scale than the master had anticipated. White Fang had observed closely the chicken-yards and the habits of the chickens. In the night-time, after they had gone to roost, he climbed to the top of a pile of newly hauled lumber. From there he gained the roof of a chicken-house, passed over the ridgepole and dropped to the ground inside. A moment later he was inside the house, and the slaughter began.

In the morning, when the master came out on to the porch, fifty white Leghorn hens, laid out in a row by" … the hired help …"greeted his eyes."

"He whistled to himself, softly, first with surprise, and then, at the end, with admiration. His eyes were likewise greeted by White Fang, but about the latter there were no signs of shame or guilt. He carried himself with pride, as though, forsooth, he had achieved a deed praiseworthy and meritorious. There was about him no consciousness of sin. The master's lips tightened as he faced the disagreeable task. Then he talked harshly to the unwitting culprit, and in his voice there was nothing but godlike wrath. Also, he held White Fang's nose down to the slain hens, and at the same time cuffed him soundly.

White Fang never raided a chicken-roost again. It was against the law, and he had learned it. Then the master took him into the chicken-yards. White Fang's natural impulse, when he saw the live food fluttering about him and under his very nose, was to spring upon it. He obeyed the impulse, but was checked by the master's voice. They continued in the yards for half an hour. Time and again the impulse surged over White Fang, and each time, as he yielded to it, he was checked by the master's voice. Thus it was he learned the law, and ere he left the domain of the chickens, he had learned to ignore their existence."

Contemplation #1

As White Fang grew closer and more entrenched in the ways of mankind, he had to learn more and more laws. Before all of this, as a cub back in the Yukon wild, the laws had been very simple: kill or be killed; eat or be eaten. Under Gray Beaver, he learned some new laws: never to bite his man-animal god and to respect and obey him. He was also to protect Gray Beaver's son Mit-sah and the property around his teepee. While he ended up getting into a lot of fights with the other dogs around the

Indian camp, he was not supposed to kill the other dogs. He also was not to bite the other man-animal gods that were not part of Gray Beaver's family (unless it was as a necessity as a guard dog). He was thus taught to restrain some of his natural inclinations. Now, under Weedon Scott, the laws he needed to learn continued to grow even more complex. Because of this, it necessitated even more learned restraint on the part of White Fang. The southland property was vast and yet it had its bounds. He needed to learn his new boundary lines. He needed to learn the new family members of Weedon Scott. He needed to be kind to the children and to be patient if they poked or prodded at him. He also needed to learn to get along with pet dogs. These were not sled dogs which he was used to, but pet dogs that were present on the property more for companionship than for work. And so it was, as his love grew for his master, he also had these additional laws to follow. And now on the southland property he needed to learn a new law – that of not eating the domesticated chickens.

In the Yukon wild, things were much simpler. But as he had grown more and more involved in the lives of man, he was needing to learn more laws. Life was more complex. And while White Fang couldn't have understood it, in reality his actual existence depended upon him learning these laws. For instance, the multiple other family members of the Scott household were rather leery of having this arctic wild wolf hound so close to the little children. If White Fang would have bitten one of the children, and we can recall what damage White Fang had done with his namesake fangs, Weedon Scott would have had a major decision regarding him. Likewise, if White

Fang did not learn the law about the chickens, Weedon Scott would again have a difficult decision to make regarding him. He could not have a dog freely run around on the property who would regularly kill the chickens that they were raising. He would have to consider chaining White Fang up or questioning if he should even live with them at all. The thing that was beyond White Fang's comprehension was that these laws, these necessary areas of learned restraint, were actually freeing. By restraining himself in his lower nature, it allowed Weedon Scott to give White Fang freedom throughout the property. By restricting his natural impulses, White Fang was allowed to freely roam. While it seemed to be restraining and limiting of his freedom, it was in actuality about achieving an even greater freedom.

For the purposes of our discussion, these experiences of White Fang could be analogous to that of the ancient Israelite people as they were leaving Egypt. Similar to White Fang living in the Yukon wild, when the Israelites were enslaved for literally centuries by the Egyptians, life was simpler. They were slaves. They knew their boundaries, they knew what they could do, they knew what they could not do. The Egyptians in power would lord over them and they did not have the ability with which to act otherwise. But with Moses and the miraculous crossing of the Red Sea under God's directed guidance, things changed. They were no longer slaves. And as a people, they were becoming closer to God through Moses and his intimate experiences with God. It was in this context in coming out of slavery that God gave the Israelite people through Moses The Ten Commandments. While they are laws that restrict various actions, they are in actuality the avenues to freedom. In this case, they are similar to White Fang who learned new laws as he became more entrenched in the lives of man which subsequently gave him more freedom. The means utilized was the same in the case of both White Fang and of the Israelite people. There needed to be a restraint of natural impulses and lower base desires to allow for greater overall freedom. The Ten Commandments again were not in actuality about restraining freedom. They were about gaining an even greater freedom. By following the laws it placed the people under the proper authority of the true God while at the same time resulting in a more harmonious interaction between the peoples themselves. And it was this positive presentation that God was trying to utilize in His chosen people to show the rest of humanity. Similar to White Fang, if the laws were not followed, then there were necessary consequences that needed to occur. If White Fang did not follow the laws and for instance bit one of the children or continued to kill the chickens, then punitive action would need to be taken and freedoms lifted. Likewise, if the Israelite people did not follow the Ten Commandments that God had given them, there would be negative consequences. And as the story proceeds from Exodus we, in fact, see this happen over and over.

So we can see the similarities between the adventures of White Fang as he moved to the southland, his new land, and to the Israelites, as they moved to the Promised Land, their new land. As White Fang grew closer and more entrenched in the ways of mankind, he had to learn more laws. As the Israelites grew closer and more entrenched in the ways of God, they had to learn more laws.

By restriction of his natural impulses, it allowed White Fang his freedom in his new surroundings. By restriction of the Israelite people of their natural impulses, it also allowed them increased freedom in their new surroundings. In both cases, while these laws seem to be restraining and limiting of freedom, in actuality they are about achieving an even greater freedom, a freedom that both had difficulty comprehending during the process.

Contemplation #2

There were chickens, 50 of them, all laid out in order. What a slaughter! The master was duly impressed. White Fang, on the other hand, was without any remorse. He did not know that he had done anything wrong! Coming from the Yukon wild, the only domesticated animal he was ever used to were other dogs. Everything else was literally fair game. The author notes:
" He carried himself with pride, as though, forsooth, he had achieved a deed praiseworthy and meritorious. There was about him no consciousness of sin." *It was then that the master's lips tightened and he talked harshly to White Fang and in his voice there was noted to be a God-like wrath. He also held White Fang's nose down to the slain hens while at the same time cuffing him soundly.*

It was later that the master then took White Fang into the chicken yards themselves. It was White Fang's natural impulse, seeing the chickens fluttering around him, to spring upon them. But he obeyed the impulse when checked by the master's voice. This went on for a half an hour. Time and again the impulse would come over White Fang and each time as he yielded to it, he was checked by the master's voice. It was in this way that he learned the law. He learned that he needed to leave the chickens alone.

It was because of his great love for his master that this law was learned. A harsh word from the master and a cuffing were much more painful to White Fang than the beatings he had previously been given by Gray Beaver or Beauty Smith. Because of his love for the master, it cut him to his core. He wanted to please the master. He wanted to keep the closeness that he knew he had with the master. It was all about love and because of this in time he was able to curb his natural impulses and learn the new law.

An analogy can be made in this case to our own humanity and God-given makeup. We have within each one of us a God given conscience, a deep inner voice calling us to do what is good and to avoid evil. It is always present with us and, if properly formed, makes itself known just at the right moment. It is our own deep inner sanctuary. So while we are learning the laws of God, a cuff is not utilized nor actual auditory sharp words as in the case of White Fang, but this deep inner voice gives its guidance or makes its indictments.

As Catholics, one is taught to undergo an examination of conscience in preparation for undertaking the sacrament of confession and reconciliation. I can think of no more interesting an example of undertaking this examination of conscience than White Fang being presented with the 50 chickens in order and the master holding White Fang's nose down to the slain hens while at the same time cuffing him soundly. For this is what we are to do during an examination of conscience. We are to consider our actions, what we should have done, what we did do, sins of omission and commission and let their severity sink in. As the cuffing of Weedon Scott to White Fang over each individual slain chicken drives home the point so does the seriousness of each sin that we have committed get impressed upon us. In order to change from our sinful ways we must first see sin for what it really is.

The master then purposefully took White Fang into the chicken yards where White Fang was presented with continuous temptation. Each time White Fang obeyed his natural impulse and would spring after a chicken, he was checked by the master's voice. This continued for half an hour and over and over as the impulse was yielded, he was checked by the master's voice. In time, he was able to learn the law. This same process is actually very similar to that which we undergo as humans in learning to avoid sin. While White Fang was purposely taken into the chicken yards to be amidst constant temptations, God has likewise placed us here on Earth, amidst our own ongoing temptations. When White Fang obeyed his natural impulse, he was checked by the master's voice. When we obey our natural impulses to temptation, we are checked by our conscience. Unfortunately, in our fallen state we often fail to follow our conscience and continue with the completion of the sinful act. And God, knowing us better than we know ourselves, has instituted a very worthwhile process to handle this. It is then that the sacrament of confession and reconciliation has its role. In going through the examination of conscience, we view even more seriously the severity of our sins. And it is with reconciliation and God's added grace that we can again go out into the world and face the temptations, this time with greater prudence and an increased awareness. And like White Fang, this process can take time and be repeated over and over again. Yet the effort is real and guided by God's grace. Like White Fang, we can eventually learn God's law.

It is important to note that it was White Fang's love for his master that motivated him when he did not do what was right. When the master disapproved, White Fang's **"spirit wilted"**. *It was not fear of punishment by his master that caused him to change his ways but because he did not want to hurt his master. We can likewise see this within the Catholic faith when we discuss the differences between perfect and imperfect contrition. If one goes to confession and is only sorry because he(she) was caught in his(her) sin and is fearful of any punishment that God could give him(her) for the sin, then this is considered imperfect contrition.*

On the other hand, if one is remorseful for the sin committed because it hurts our loving God and damages that personal relationship then this is considered perfect contrition. While imperfect contrition is certainly valid and worthwhile, perfect contrition is the much preferred way to go. But this in part depends upon the personal relationship and closeness to God to start with. In the case of White Fang, he had developed a strong love for Weedon Scott and his contrition would be considered perfect contrition rather than imperfect. He wasn't just trying to avoid punishment and in fact the punishment given to him with the cuffing by Weedon Scott was actually quite mild. It was that it hurt their close relationship that was so bothersome to White Fang.

DAVID G. SMITHSON, MD

With his great love for his master he changed his ways and learned the law. Likewise, as our growth in our relationship with God strengthens and deepens, we can better overcome sin and more fully learn His laws.

CHAPTER 10

PURPOSEFUL TEMPTATION

"'You can never cure a chicken-killer.' Judge Scott shook his head sadly at the luncheon table, when his son narrated the lesson he had given White Fang. 'Once they've got the habit and the taste of blood …' Again he shook his head sadly.

But Weedon Scott did not agree with his father. 'I'll tell you what I'll do,' he challenged finally. 'I'll lock White Fang in the with the chickens all afternoon.'

'But think of the chickens,' objected the Judge.

'And furthermore,' the son went on, 'for every chicken he kills, I'll pay you one dollar gold coin of the realm.'

'But you should penalize father, too,' interposed Beth.

Her sister seconded her, and a chorus of approval arose from around the table. Judge Scott nodded his head in agreement.

'All right.' Weedon Scott pondered for a moment. 'And if, at the end of the afternoon, White Fang hasn't harmed a chicken, for every ten minutes of the time he has spent in the yard, you will have to say to him, gravely and with deliberation, just as if you were sitting on the bench and solemnly passing judgement, 'White Fang, you are smarter than I thought.'

From hidden points of vantage the family watched the performance. But it was a fizzle. Locked in the yard and there deserted by the master, White Fang lay down and went to sleep. Once he got up and walked over to the trough for a drink of water. The chickens he calmly ignored. So far as he was concerned they did not exist. At four o'clock he executed a running jump, gained the roof of the chicken house and leaped to the ground outside, whence he sauntered gravely to the house. He had learned the law. And on the porch, before the delighted family, Judge Scott, face to face with White Fang, said slowly and solemnly, sixteen times, 'White Fang, you are smarter than I thought.'

Contemplation

As Weedon Scott purposefully allowed temptation for White Fang, so also God can purposefully allow temptation for mankind. In the story of Job, God specifically grants Satan the opportunity to test Job. Jesus Himself was led by the Holy Spirit into the wilderness in order to be tempted by the devil. And stories abound with the saints in this regard. White Fang was locked in with the chickens and left by the master. He knew not why. All he knew was that he was intimately surrounded by temptation. Job was living a life as a wealthy man with a large family and extensive flocks. He was noted to be blameless and upright. And then, one day, everything changes. He ends up losing everything. In the course of the entire book Job is asking why. Jesus, as both God and man, was nevertheless tempted by the devil in His humanity. And the stories of the saints are again rich with temptations encountered.

If we look on the other hand of the equation, however, Weedon Scott had a purpose as to why he was tempting White Fang. And God, likewise, has a purpose as to why He allows us to be tempted. For White Fang, it was a test. For Job, it was a test as well as for our Lord and the many saints. It may be a growth process that one needs to go through in preparation for events to come. For our Lord, it may have been an initiation, a process of strengthening the will in preparation for the intense temptations He would be undergoing during His public years and especially as He approached His passion. Like White Fang, we may never know why we are placed at times in such difficult situations of temptation. Could these times of difficult temptation also be allowed by God for our own callings or undertakings? Either way, we must stay the course and stay close to God as we weather the storm.

Chapter 11

Random Temptation

"Life was complex in the Santa Clara Valley after the simplicities of the Northland. And the chief thing demanded by these intricacies of civilization was control, restraint – a poise of self that was as delicate as the fluttering of gossamer wings and at the same time as rigid as steel. Life had a thousand faces, and White Fang found he must meet them all – thus, when he went to town, into San Jose, running behind the carriage or loafing about the streets when the carriage stopped. Life flowed past him, deep and wide and varied, continually impinging upon his senses, demanding of him instant and endless adjustments and correspondences, and compelling him, almost always, to suppress his natural impulses.

There were butcher-shops where meat hung within reach. This meat he must not touch. There were cats at the houses the master visited that must be let alone. And there were dogs everywhere that snarled at him and that he must not attack. And then, on the crowded sidewalks, there were persons innumerable whose attention he attracted. They would stop and look at him, point him out to one another, examine him, talk to him, and worse of all, pat him. And these perilous contacts from all these strange hands he must endure. Yet this endurance he achieved…"

Contemplation

In the last chapter we discussed how White Fang was purposefully taken to the chicken yards by his master in order to be tempted. In this chapter, the discussion is more about random temptations. There are the butcher shops where meat hung down within reach. There are the cats, the dogs and the crowded sidewalks with innumerable people. He was continuously assailed by constant temptation. So it is with us in our world. There is the ongoing assault to our senses, the impingement on our peace and wellbeing. With our virtual world it is even more so with the continuous ads, pop-ups, spam and various other intrusions. Due to our fallen natures, we are weakened by sin and at risk for further slip ups. Even with frequent confession and reconciliation, a wonderful grace given to Catholics by Christ when He started the church, we still need to be prudent and guarded in our actions. For while confession and reconciliation can forgive our sins and strengthen us with God's grace, the "stain" of sin is still present. The tendency is still there and our brains have neurochemical channels that remember the pathway. We typically form habit patterns of sin as sin in and of itself has a repetitive nature. We need to be forward thinking in altering these habit patterns from bad habits to good habits. The goal is to move from habits of sin to habits of virtue. We must fill our lives so much with the good that there is no room for the bad. We must further educate our conscience in the ways of truth and beauty. It is important to always be on the alert. But most of all, we must remain close to Christ. We can frequent the mass to gain grace from His Eucharistic presence. As our focus moves upward, our habit patterns change for the better. Like White Fang, we will be able to suppress those natural impulses in favor of a greater and more satisfying good. As White Fang did this for the love of his master, so we do it for the love of our God. And like White Fang, we will be able to endure those constant impingements as we deepen the loving relationship with our God.

Chapter 12

The Walls Come Down

"But it was the multiplicity of laws that befuddled White Fang and often brought him into disgrace. He had to learn that he must not touch the chickens that belonged to other gods. Then there were cats, and rabbits, and turkeys; all these he must let alone. In fact, when he had but partly learned the law, his impression was he must leave all live things alone. Out in the back-pasture, a quail could flutter up under his nose unharmed. All tense and trembling with eagerness and desire, he mastered his instinct and stood still. He was obeying the will of the gods.

And then, one day, again out in the back-pasture, he saw Dick start a jackrabbit and run it. The master himself was looking on and did not interfere. Nay, he encouraged White Fang to join in the chase. And thus he learned that there was no taboo on jackrabbits. In the end he worked out the complete law. Between him and all domestic animals there must be no hostilities. If not amity, at least neutrality must obtain. But the other animals – the squirrels, and quail and cottontails, were creatures of the Wild who had never yielded allegiance to man. They were the lawful prey of any dog. It was only the tame that the gods protected, and between the tame deadly strife was not permitted. The gods held the power of life and death over their subjects, and the gods were jealous of their power.

Contemplation

To this point, White Fang's journey was one of restraint. It was continued restraint of his natural impulses in order to have a joyful, loving relationship with his master. He needed to have restraint in areas of his life in accordance with the laws that he had learned. With regard to other animals, his impression from this learning process was that he was to leave all other animals alone and unharmed. What he realized, however, was that this applied only between him and domestic animals. The other animals, however, the squirrels, quail and cottontails were creatures of the wild who had never been tamed by man. It was these animals that were lawful prey. The master himself not only allowed this, but encouraged it. There were thus certain areas of his life where he was not only not inhibited but actually encouraged to follow his natural impulses.

With White Fang's initial learning of the multiple laws there were in place walls of restraint which existed in multiple areas of his life. These were walls where he needed to inhibit his natural impulses as per the laws which the master had instituted. In other areas, however, and specifically in the area of wild animals that had not been domesticated, he did not need to restrain his natural impulses. That wall of restraint was down. He was free to enjoy, to carefully stalk the squirrel and at once spring into action, racing at top speed in the thrill of the chase. His body was, after all, made for action. His eyes were made to closely observe the squirrel he was stalking. His attention allowed him to fully focus so he could prepare for the pounce. His back legs with their strong muscles could propel him forward and his coordinated movements involved all four extremities as he quickly traversed the landscape. Lastly, there was his strong, powerful jaw and sharp fangs which seized the victim as it attempted to run away. This is what he was naturally made for. His body, mind, form and function were geared for this.

Thus we can see that while White Fang's life was full of walls of restraint that were in place due to the laws of his master, in this area he was not only free but encouraged to loosen himself from restraint, to release his inhibitions and to enjoy fully the sensations and satisfactions of the hunt.

In a likewise manner, we humans have many walls of restraint due to God's laws that inhibit us. Like White Fang, those laws are in place for our own good. And like White Fang, we must restrain from breaking those laws. But life is more than just restraint. It is more than just inhibiting action and holding back natural impulses. Like White Fang, we also are made for action. Our hands have incredible dexterity with the capacity for strong, yet delicate, movement. They are made to help others, to make things, to be constructive. Our feet are made for walking, for bringing things to others, to move us productively from one place to another. Our tactile sense allows us to touch the delicate petals of a flower while our nose can smell the wonderful scent. The sense of taste enables us to enjoy a delicious meal. Our ears make possible the hearing of the wonderful sounds of nature, for listening to beautiful music.

Life is not all about restraint. There is not an imposition of laws strangling us into repression and resentment. No, we are made for action, for proper action within these laws. It is there that we can release our true inner nature. These things God not only allows, but encourages.

Work itself can be a source of sanctification. The daily labors and drudgery, even the frustrations and difficulties can be handled in a way that brings us closer to God. Volunteering the use of our time in service is another way. This can include practicing charity toward others. We can take the opportunity to use our skills or abilities to help those in need.

The sacrament of marriage is an example. It is within the marital covenant that God has placed the beautiful gift of sexuality. With the total self-giving of each marital partner, husband and wife, in a life-long commitment, there can be the complete and proper expression of this gift. There can be the full enjoyment and satisfaction of its benefits without any feelings of guilt or lament. Its basic purpose is two-fold: to deepen the intimacy and love of the couple, and for the miracle of procreation.

Holy leisure is another important facet of this discussion. Leisure is not to be a time when we degrade back into sinful ways, which only binds us and makes us miserable and in the end can threaten our salvation. Enjoying the outdoors, pleasurable hobbies, good conversation with friends, reading a good book, and exercise in moderation are just a few examples. Even prayer itself is work and there needs to be healthy leisure to maintain a proper balance of body, mind and spirit. It is here where beautiful symphonies are composed and tasteful artwork painted or sculpted. It is here where we can bring beauty to life and our creative juices are allowed and encouraged to flow. We are made for expression and not repression. We are made for action and not inaction. And it is within these protected walls of God's laws that it can be done with inner joy and compassion. It can be done without regret or remorse. These laws of behavior were created for our own benefit, to free us in how we express our humanity. They were given as a gift to help us live joyful, harmonious lives under His protection.

As White Fang could feel the thrill of the chase as he tracked down a squirrel with the encouragement of his master, so also can we feel the joys of our own expression with the encouragement of our God.

CHAPTER 13

SCENES OF LIFE

Life continued at Sierra Vista. Things were good. The weather was nice. There was plenty of food and the area was wide and free to roam. Weedon Scott would frequently ride out into the back pastures on horseback and White Fang would run alongside him. One time, a jack rabbit scampered quickly under the horse's feet resulting in a stumble and fall. Scott's leg was trapped and broken as the horse went down. It was very painful to move and he commanded White Fang to go back home. At first White Fang was very reluctant to leave the master and was unsure what he was asking. But he knew the word "home" and knew it was the master's will that he go home.

After returning home, the family members were quite alarmed at White Fang's behavior. He was growing savage, began barking, pacing back and forth toward the pasture. For a time they thought he was mad and Judge Scott was even more suspicious. After all, he was a wild wolf from the northland. He then pulled at the master's wife's dress. She had an instinct that something was wrong with Weedon. And thus, they followed him out into the back pasture. After this, they were all even more appreciative of White Fang and more trusting of his behavior around the property. Even Judge Scott, with all his time rendering sentences to criminals, was starting to warm to him.

Collie was a constant nuisance for White Fang, continually barking at him, cutting him off at times, not giving him peace. She still thought he was a wolf from the wild. His best way to handle her was to close his eyes and pretend he was sleeping. In time, however, she took a liking to him. One day her actions to him were actually playful. She was motioning for him to head out into the wilder parts of the property. And with her playfulness, he actually forgot that she had made life a burden to him. So she led him off on a long chase through the back pasture and well into the woods. It was there that they took a certain pathway traveled so many times before, that same pathway traveled long ago by his mother Kiche and One-Eye in the quiet northland wilderness…

It was around this time period that a convict escaped from the San Quinton prison. This convict had been sentenced by Judge Scott and sent to prison. The convict's name was Jim Hall. Unknown to anyone but the convict himself was his solitary desire to seek vengeance on Judge Scott. The Scott family heard about his escape from all the papers. The whole area was on alarm with a convict on the loose.

Regarding any of this, of course, White Fang was unaware. Now dogs were not allowed to stay in the house, but a secret developed between the master's wife, Alice, and White Fang. Each evening she would quietly let White Fang into the house and each morning she would get up early and let White Fang back out. As it so happened, one night, Jim Hall eventually found the Scott home and snuck silently through the door, well-armed, to complete his morbid task. The Judge and the rest of the extended family were all sleeping in the bedrooms upstairs. In a slow, quiet, lurking fashion, Hall started mounting the stairs going up. White Fang lay silently, watching his every move. He knew the importance of surprise in an attack.

As Hall carefully lifted his foot to the next step, White Fang sprang into action. He attacked Hall in the back and buried his fangs into the back of his neck. In the pitch black quiet, Hall and White Fang both fell backwards off the steps with a huge racket. Multiple gunshots went off. There was snarling and screams of horror. There was fighting and growling and smashing of glass and furniture. The whole household arose. The lights were turned on and the sounds quickly diminished. All that was left was a raspy, gurgling noise and no other. As Judge Scott and Weedon Scott traversed down the stairway, revolvers in hand, they witnessed the scene. The man was dead. A gaping throat wound was the cause. As the Judge looked into the face, he recognized that of Jim Hall. He and Weedon shared a significant glance. Turning next to White Fang, they noted he was bleeding from multiple areas. Some of his limbs were deformed. His eyes were barely open and his was weakly gasping for air.

As outside help was called in, the author continues with the tale:

"'Frankly, he has one chance in a thousand,' announced the surgeon, after he had worked an hour and a half on White Fang.

'One broken hind-leg,' he went on. 'Three broken ribs, one at least of which has pierced the lungs. He has lost nearly all the blood in his body. There is a large likelihood of internal injuries…to say nothing of the three bullet holes clear through him. He hasn't a chance in ten thousand,'

'But he mustn't lose any chance that might be of help to him', Judge Scott exclaimed. Never mind expense…'

The surgeon smiled indulgently. 'Of course I understand. He deserves all that can be done for him. He must be nursed as you would nurse a human being, a sick child. And don't forget what I told you about temperature. I'll be back at ten o'clock again.'

White Fang received the nursing. Judge Scott's suggestion of a trained nurse was indignantly clamored down by the girls, who themselves undertook the task. And White Fang won out on the one chance in ten thousand denied him by the surgeon…

Bound down a prisoner, denied even movement by the plaster casts and bandages, White Fang lingered out the weeks. He slept long hours and dreamed much, and through his mind passed an unending pageant of Northland visions. All the ghosts of the past arose and were with him. Once again he lived in the lair with Kiche, crept trembling to the knees of Gray Beaver to tender his allegiance, ran for his life before Lip-Lip and all the howling bedlam of the puppy-pack.

He ran again through the silence, hunting his living food through the months of famine; and again he ran at the head of the team, the gut-whips of Mit-sah and Gray Beaver snapping behind, their voices crying, 'Raa! Raa!' when they came to a narrow passage and the team closed together like a fan to go through. He lived again all his days with Beauty Smith and the fights he had fought. At such times he whimpered and snarled in his sleep, and they that looked on said that his dreams were bad.

But there was one particular nightmare from which he suffered – the clanking, clanging monsters of electric cars that were to him colossal screaming lynxes. He would lie in a screen of bushes, watching for a squirrel to venture far enough out on the ground from its tree-refuge. Then, when he sprang out upon it, it would transform itself into an electric car, menacing and terrible, towering over him like a mountain, screaming and clanging and spitting fire at him. It was the same when he challenged the hawk down out of the sky. Down out of the blue it would rush, as it dropped upon him changing itself into the ubiquitous electric car. Or again, he would be in the pen of Beauty Smith. Outside the pen, men would be gathering, and he knew that a fight was on. He watched the door for his antagonist to enter. The door would open, and thrust in upon him would come the awful electric car. A thousand times this occurred, and each time the terror it inspired was as vivid and great as ever..."

The Parable of White Fang

Contemplation

With multiple traumatic injuries and several through and through bullet wounds, White Fang was laying literally at death's door. It was during his prolonged recuperation that he relives his life experiences; starting as a cub in the wild, through his times in the Indian camp with Gray Beaver, through the horrible dog fights while caged by Beauty Smith, to his most recent life in the Santa Clara Valley. Things get intriguing with the repetitive, horrific nightmare involving the huge, menacing electric car. Over and over this nightmare occurs, dreadful and terrible with each frightful episode. Was this representative of some type of post traumatic physical and emotional ordeal from the multiple horrible experiences throughout much of his life? After all, he had battled for survival as a cub while the rest of his birth litter had died, he was frequently picked on as a cub by the rest of the puppy pack at the Indian camp, he was viciously abused in the worst way by Beauty Smith, he had struggled through enormous odds to achieve his happier current existence and now had just went through major life threatening trauma in defending those he cared for at Sierra Vista. Was this recurring nightmare an unfortunate and painful emotional byproduct, a side effect of all of this trauma? Could it subsequently result in a type of release, a letting go, a process of healing from all of the physical and emotional wrongdoing that had been done to him?

Furthermore, what is the role of all of these scenes of life being played out before White Fang anyway? He literally has his life experiences pass before him as he is down and close to death. Are they representative of some type of assessment of White Fang's life? Could they be illustrative of a type of final judgement? It's hard to know in retrospect exactly what the author was thinking when he wrote this, but it certainly allows a lot of room for conjecture and supposition.

Chapter 14

Joyful Triumph

"Then came the day when the last bandage and the last plaster cast were taken off. It was a gala day. All Sierra Vista was gathered around. The master rubbed his ears, and he crooned his love-growl. The master's wife called him the 'Blessed Wolf,' which name was taken up with acclaim and all the women called him the 'Blessed Wolf.'

He tried to rise to his feet, and after several attempts fell down from weakness. He had lain so long that his muscles had lost their cunning, and all the strength had gone out of them. He felt a little shame because of his weakness, as though, forsooth, he were failing the gods in the service he owed them. Because of this he made heroic efforts to arise, and at last he stood on his four legs, tottering and swaying back and forth.

'The Blessed Wolf!' chorused the women.

Judge Scott surveyed them triumphantly.

'Out of your own mouths be it,' he said. 'Just as I contended right along. No mere dog could have done what he did. He's a wolf.'

'A Blessed Wolf,' amended the Judge's wife.

'Yes, Blessed Wolf,' agreed the Judge. 'And henceforth that shall be my name for him.'

'He'll have to learn to walk again,' said the surgeon; 'so he might as well start in right now. It won't hurt him. Take him outside.'

And outside he went, like a king, with all Sierra Vista about him and tending on him. He was very weak, and when he reached the lawn he lay down and rested for a while.

Then the procession started on, little spurts of strength coming into White Fang's muscles as he used them and the blood began to surge through them. The stables were reached, and there in the doorway lay Collie, a half-dozen pudgy puppies playing about her in the sun.

White Fang looked on with a wondering eye. Collie snarled warningly at him, and he was careful to keep his distance. The master with his toe helped one sprawling puppy toward him. He bristled suspiciously, but the master warned him that all was well. Collie, clasped in the arms of one of the women, watched him jealously and with a snarl warned him that all was not well.

The puppy sprawled in front of him. He cocked his ears and watched it curiously. Then their noses touched, and he felt the warm little tongue of the puppy on his jowl. White Fang's tongue went out, he knew not why, and he licked the puppy's face.

Hand-clapping and pleased cries from the gods greeted the performance. He was surprised, and looked at them in a puzzled way. Then his weakness asserted itself, and he lay down, his ears cocked, his head on one side, as he watched the puppy. The other puppies came sprawling toward him, to Collie's great disgust; and he gravely permitted them to clamber and tumble over him... the puppies' antics and mauling continued, and he lay with half-shut, patient eyes, drowsing in the sun.

Contemplation

In this final chapter there is the celebration of the long, at times very difficult, but in the end, wonderfully successful journey of White Fang's life. He had passed the test. In striving for obedience, he could be considered to have, "ran the race," to paraphrase Saint Paul, or to have, "fought the good fight." He tried to put his master first in his life, even to the point of a near martyrdom in his master's defense. The reward was the wonderful celebration described in the above chapter. It could almost be considered what Heaven would be as depicted for a dog. It was a true family event, with the little puppies adding even more joy.

White Fang was given a new name, "Blessed Wolf." This same term, "Blessed," is used for mankind when on the pathway to sainthood. Yes, yes, he had made it. Likewise, we are called to do the same in our own way. As taming of the animal enables it to be a companion and instrument of service to man, so also growing in holiness enables man to be a companion and instrument of service to God. As taming of the animal enables it to live in the house of man, so does growth in holiness enable man to live in the house of God. Like White Fang striving for obedience and closeness to his master, we are to strive for holiness and closeness to our God. As White Fang, "ran the race," and, "fought the good fight," to learn the laws of man in pleasing his master, we are to do the same in learning the laws of God who is our master. And like White Fang, who was receptive to his master's teachings, we are called to be receptive to God's teachings.

Dogs are not made in man's image as both are creatures. But, as we have seen, because of their intelligence and potential amiability they have been found to be good human companions and can serve very useful human means. The goal of the dog in this case is domestication in the human household and becoming "one of the family."

Man, however, was made in God's image and we are "partakers of the divine nature" (2 Peter 1:4). We are called from the first to come eventually into our true home, heaven, which is God's house. We are called to follow God's pathway, as difficult and as challenging as that may be, to achieve our true destination. It is God's house, becoming one of "God's family", with all the angels and saints, where there are many rooms and where Christ has gone to individually prepare a place for us. This is our true home where we can achieve lasting and eternal joy and happiness. This is our final aim, the goal seeing us through all of our trials. It is God's house and for each one of us, it is the ultimate domestication.

Notes

1. Stephenson, Robert Louis, *Treasure Island,* Reader's Digest Best Loved Books for Young Readers, Vol 1, The Reader's Digest Association, Pleasantville, NY, 1966.

2. Dickens, Charles, *David Copperfield,* Reader's Digest Best Loved Books for Young Readers, Vol. 1, The Reader's Digest Association, Pleasantville, NY,1966.

3. London, Jack, *Call of the Wild,* Reader's Digest Best Loved Books for Young Readers, Vol. 1, The Reader's Digest Association, Pleasantville, NY, 1966.

4. London, Jack, *White Fang*, The MacMillan Company, Norwood Press, Norwood, MA, 1906.

5. Peter Kreeft, *Making Sense Out Of Suffering*, Servant Books, Ann Arbor, MI, 1986, pp158-159.

6. Gabel, Stewart, *Jack London: A Man In Search Of Meaning, A Jungian Perspective,* AuthorHouse, 2012, pp14.

7. Smith, Warren Allen, *Whose Who In Hell, A Handbook And International Directory For Humanists, Freethinkers, Naturalists, Rationalists and Non-theists*, Barricade Books, Ft. Lee, NJ, 2000.

8. Miho Nagasawa, Shouhei Mitsui, Shirori En, Nobuyo, Mitsuaki Ohta, Yasuo Sakuma, Tatsushi Onaka, Kazutaka Mogi, Takefumi Kikusui, <u>Oxytocin-gaze positive loop and the coevolution of human-dog bonds</u>, Science 17 April 2015: Vol. 348 no. 6232 pp. 333-336. This study from Japan indicated that when dogs and humans gaze lovingly into one another's eyes, each of their brains secretes oxytocin – a hormone linked to maternal bonding and trust. This is a type of hormone that is also seen between mother and child and between mates. Human/dog is the only case in which it has been observed between two different species (sorry cat lovers!).

Author Biography

Dr. David Smithson was born and raised in Winona, Minnesota. As an undergraduate, he worked in medical research at the Mayo Clinic in Rochester, Minnesota, and graduated from Saint Mary's University of Minnesota with studies in chemistry and biology. He completed medical school at the University of Minnesota in Minneapolis. His internship was at the Gundersen Clinic/La Crosse Lutheran Hospital, La Crosse, Wisconsin. His residency was completed at the University of Washington in Seattle where he specialized in physical medicine and rehabilitation. Dr. Smithson is board certified in physical medicine and rehabilitation. He has practiced in the Kansas City area since 1990 and is the medical director of inpatient rehabilitation services at St. Joseph Medical Center. He directs the rehabilitation care of patients with strokes, head injuries, spinal cord injury, amputations, and complex medical cases, etc.

On a personal side, Dr. Smithson and his wife, Mollie, have been married for over 30 years. They have five children and two grandchildren. They are parishioners at Queen of the Holy Rosary Catholic Church in Wea, Kansas, where Dr. Smithson is a lector, a member of the

Knights of Columbus, and a member of the men's Catholic faith group. He has given talks locally and through the Archdiocese of Kansas City, Kansas on the topics of habit and virtue with coverage in the Archdiocesan newspaper *The Leaven*. He is a lifelong dog lover and dog owner.

ACKNOWLEDGMENTS

To my wonderful wife, Mollie, for your great support and encouragement, for your understanding when I would frequently wake up in the middle of the night with book ideas that needed to be recorded, for being the love of my life, my innermost companion, and also for helping with editing!

To Lari, my administrative assistant, for your quick wit and hardy laugh; you have great organizational and communication skills. How could I go wrong hiring a former math teacher!

To Dr. John Morris and the many supportive members of the Ethics Committee at St. Joseph Medical Center in Kansas City.

To Bob Triano, Grand Knight of Council #12546, Queen of the Holy Rosary of Wea, for your words of encouragement and support with the Knights of Columbus.

To Lenny Vohs and the many supportive men of the Saturday morning faith gatherings.

To Father Gary Pennings, pastor of Queen of the Holy Rosary of Wea and Vicar General of the Archdiocese of Kansas City, Kansas, for your support of this project.

Most of all, I would like to thank God, for His initial idea, frequent insights, remarkable vision of beauty, and final push to get this thing done.

www.ingramcontent.com/pod-product-compliance
Lightning Source LLC
Chambersburg PA
CBHW070926080526
44589CB00013B/1437